Christ Cult Codex

The Secrets of the Abrahamic Religions

Dan Desmarques

22 Lions

Christ Cult Codex: The Secrets of the Abrahamic Religions

Written by Dan Desmarques

Contents

Introduction

This book aims to expose the layers of deception and control that have shaped religious beliefs and practices for centuries, influencing the lives of billions of people worldwide.

As you embark on this journey, you will encounter a critical examination of the foundations of the Abrahamic religions, historical and contemporary interpretations of key figures and events, and the profound impact these beliefs have had on society. You will explore the origins of monotheistic ideologies, the role of extraterrestrial interference in shaping religious narratives, and the manipulative tactics used by religious institutions to maintain control over their followers.

The Christ Cult Codex seeks to empower readers by providing them with the knowledge and tools necessary to question and challenge the dogmas that have long been accepted without question. By piercing the veil of ignorance and unraveling the deceptions that permeate religious teachings, we can begin to awaken our consciousness and set ourselves on the path to true enlightenment and spiritual liberation.

This book is not merely an academic exercise; it is a call to action. It encourages readers to think critically, to question authority, and to seek truth beyond the confines of religious doctrine. By understanding the historical and contemporary contexts of religious beliefs, we can better navigate the complexities of our world and work toward a more just and compassionate society. Explore the dark side of faith and power, the hidden secrets of religious institutions, and the potential for ascension beyond the confines of the Christ cult. With this book, you can uncover the truth and forge a new path to spiritual awakening and liberation.

Chapter 1: Abraham Decoded

The Abrahamic religions are practiced today by an estimated 4 billion people, about half the world's population. This means that many of our values, choices, and thoughts are conditioned by what these religions promote. Yet few dare to question their validity, despite the fact that they have perpetuated conflict, genocide, and the eradication of numerous civilizations over thousands of years, all in the name of a deity.

Those capable of higher consciousness will see the truth and find it liberating, while those still trapped by the lure of the Abrahamic religions will remain in darkness. We have been warned by many prophets of the lies that would lead us astray from the truth. Humanity has been deceived and manipulated, used and abused in the name of a falsehood that has far-reaching consequences for how we shape our world.

As a planetary race, we can only continue to evolve if we educate ourselves and stop creating wars that are never justified when promoted in the name of a false god. Although the truth may be shocking, it will also reveal much about our hidden nature and lead to our spiritual liberation. This freedom from the shackles of dogma will, in time, allow for a greater and more evolved planetary consciousness.

Humans have always needed a prophet or guru to bridge their understanding of the Divine. In some cases such prophets have been called God reincarnated. Christ was not the first figure to be seen in this way. However, the distortions and misunderstandings that have accumulated around the teachings of Jesus have reached a point where few today can truly understand their purpose. The type of Christianity that has been popularized is more in line with ancient Roman values and political views than with the words of Jesus. We can see this in a conversation between Christ and Judas, where Jesus tells him (in the Gospel of Judas): "Lift up your eyes and look at the cloud and the light in it and the stars around it. The star that leads the way is your star".

With this phrase, Jesus presents himself as a teacher of the collective consciousness expressed in the entire universe. For he was not unique in his words, but rather a representative of that consciousness manifested in many other galaxies and planets. However, like any other popular teacher, his words were later corrupted to reinforce agendas designed to manipulate the masses. Following this phrase, we see that "Judas lifted up his eyes and saw the shining cloud, and he entered into it" (in the Gospel of Judas).

The evidence for extraterrestrial contact is abundant in the interactions between Jesus and the angels. Yet many Christians today insist on depicting angels as winged beings, a linear depiction used to explain the existence of people from other galaxies.

Although many Christians today scoff at the possibility that their angels are just people from other planets, here we have a reference to Jesus and Judas joining angels in a spaceship and traveling around the universe to gain more wisdom. So why would Judas betray Jesus? He didn't! Jesus saw the body as an obstacle to his ascension. He was trying to escape death until his work on earth was complete, and when it was, his death was welcome. The same Gospel shows us this when Jesus says to Judas: "You will sacrifice the one who clothes me".

Jesus' death, with the help of Judas, would free his spirit to unite with the brotherhood from which he came. Jesus was a Starseed and an Avatar. He was one of many who have come to Earth throughout our history, and even more so in recent years, to share the teachings of advanced civilizations. The true teachings of Jesus are consistent with the teachings of others who, like him, have sought to represent the collective at higher levels of existence. When we compare these teachings with many others rooted in the same truth of galactic consciousness, we see that they speak the same, no matter how much the masses still disbelieve, thousands of years later.

There are three types of apparitions associated with angels: extraterrestrials of either benign or malevolent nature; souls of deceased people; and holographic or artificial manifestations stimulated by hypnosis or the use of drugs. There are no other types of angels except those in these groups. So when people claim to see angels, as shown in Christian pamphlets, they are probably dealing with angels of the third kind, which can be created by the first group or even by earthly technology.

The use of drugs can also be used by either earthly groups or extraterrestrials to accomplish agendas through induced hallucinations. The Book of Revelation, which has such a tormenting effect on the psyche of many Christians, is an example of a writing by a man high on extraterrestrial hallucinogenic drugs.

Chapter 2: Revelation Unveiled

In Revelation 10:8-11, John tells us: "The voice that I heard from heaven spoke to me again, saying, 'Go and take the little scroll that is opened in the hand of the angel who stands on the sea and on the earth. So I went to the angel and said to him, 'Give me the little scroll. And he said to me, "Take it and eat it, and it will make your belly bitter, but in your mouth it will be sweet as honey. And I took the little scroll out of the angel's hand, and I ate it; and it was in my mouth as sweet as honey; and when I had eaten it, my belly was bitter."

This passage describes John being drugged before being shown images of an apocalyptic nature. These visions had nothing to do with facts, but were merely photographs or artificially created drawings that someone today could create with a computer. We must not assume that people at that time could tell the difference. If it's easy to fool people today with artificial intelligence, it would certainly be easier in a time when the technology was not available. In fact, if John had seen an apocalyptic movie through a television screen, he would have believed it was real because they had no idea what a television was.

Movies are so realistic that most people in today's world often have difficulty distinguishing reality from fiction. This lack of discernment stems from a natural predisposition in the human psyche to fantasy. Religion was built on the ignorance of the many and took advantage of this mental predisposition because such ignorance favored the control of the few. Many others failed to do the same and were therefore segregated into the realms of the occult, as if the Abrahamic religions were somehow more truthful than others.

If ever there was a true religion in the world, it was surely the one that came directly from the gods. I am referring to the Egyptian religion, which is the one from which all the occult branches drink their knowledge, namely the Rosicrucians, the Freemasons, and even Wicca. Everything else was created to deceive the masses of society, who are always susceptible to fairy tales and imaginary stories. But fairy tales have to evolve over time, and that's what the Abrahamic religions are - a more elaborate, effective, and complex fantasy.

It is not possible to get people to accept a religion whose abstract meanings are too far removed from their limited and mundane minds. The religion of the dull must be at the same level as their intellectual potential. This is why so many truths have been lost in the course of time; they either did not interest the many or provoked them negatively. Those who spoke such truths were persecuted, ridiculed, and murdered. And nothing has changed since then; speaking the truth is still met with threats, insults, and murder.

If I use my own books as a comparison to evaluate these statements, the same can be seen. Most people look at these books and barely understand them, or they think I'm making up what I know, that I can't possibly be enlightened or know more than those they worship, as if their ego is the ruler of truth. Many people I meet even tell me that I don't look like a writer, which is very interesting since I have published hundreds of books and have more than 100 Amazon bestsellers, many of them number one. Yet they think that facts mean nothing compared to their stereotypes. If reality isn't real except through the filter of the masses, what can we say about religion?

People want to put the whole universe into a little marble that they can put in their pocket and call their own. Their ego is so big that they can't fit anything significant into their heads. They then call their lies truth and disregard the truth as if it were a lie. So why is it so hard to understand that aliens are more interested in studying our ignorance than in communicating with us? They are interested in studying our stupidity because there are not many people on Earth with the brains to make decisions that are relevant and effective for the whole of society. But no leader can do more than what people are willing to accept and assimilate as their own. In fact, society never supports such individuals, even when they appear in public and there is such an opportunity. Instead, people choose leaders who meet their expectations, and if they could choose my profession, I would obviously not be able to become a writer.

The vast majority of people don't have the ability to see reality and truth in its entirety, and that's what enlightenment is - it's the ability to see things as they are and in their entirety. When people move away from seeing reality as it is because they want to be in their own bubble and they can't handle the rotten facts and the disgusting things that go on in other people's minds, they cannot be enlightened. Many would say that they would like to read other people's minds, but if they could, they would be depressed knowing what goes on in their minds. Many would say that not everyone is like that, and that there are a lot of good people in the world, but even though that may be true, you don't grow a whole field of potatoes to get a good one out of all the rotten ones.

Chapter 3: Ignorance Pierced

In recent years, many truths have come to the surface. We have been blessed in recent decades with a tremendous wealth of information, much of it coming from archaeological discoveries and the recovery of lost books. Despite this, we still have many liars in the world, and they have a lot of power to make sure that people don't have access to what has been found. The problem with contradictory information is that it makes those who have a dualistic way of analyzing reality even more confused than before. Because such people can't understand what contradicts itself, they can't think for themselves because of their own intellectual misery - built on an educational system that indoctrinates, segregates and discriminates against those who can think for themselves.

The majority of the population lacks discernment, analytical potential, and the courage to be different, and without these they can't see the truth in front of them. When such people meet someone like me, they think I am the liar and everything else they have heard before is the truth. Because of the dual mindset of the masses, they have to take the pieces as a whole and choose sides because they can't analyze anything that puts them in a state of cognitive dissonance. The psychopaths of this planet know this, which is why they destroy the credibility of any new information by promoting such dissonance.

For example, when Ivermectin was proposed as a cure for coronavirus, the greedy, fearful of losing the profits they were making from the ignorance of the masses, rushed to claim that there was no scientific evidence of its efficacy and that it was better suited for treating horses. By increasing the cognitive dissonance of the masses, they were easily able to destroy the credibility of this cheap, award-winning, and very effective remedy.

The problem with ignorance is that it protects itself from disappearing by strengthening the ego. The ignorant always merge their personality with their own ignorance. And when that ignorance is threatened, they defend it as if it were a war for survival. In this state of mind, many become violent, even when the violence isn't justified. In ancient times people fought to protect their lives, but now people fight all the time because they are stupid and immature.

The prophets who came to earth wanted to dissolve this stupidity, and what did the masses do? They huddled together in small groups where they could cultivate and maintain their fantasies as an impenetrable body of beliefs called religion. The real problem with religion is that no matter how open the members claim to be, as soon as you prove them wrong, you are ridiculed, insulted, and ostracized. They are open to the extent that you are stupid enough not to ask questions they can't answer. That's the limit of their sympathy and compassion.

It would be the same as meeting a psychopath and expecting him to be kind to you. The psychopath will be kind as long as there are consequences to his behavior. In fact, it is only the fear of punishment that keeps society under the apparent illusion of order. If the ATMs suddenly stopped spitting out money, and the police and military disappeared at the same time, you would see the most brutal chaos in history unfold before your very eyes. People like me are on this planet to make sure that consciousness rises to a level where that can't happen, but there is a long way to go before that state is reached.

There is only one truth and there are many ways to reach it, just as there are many ways to speak the same words in different languages. With each language we find different meanings and ways of structuring phrases, but the intention can remain the same, just as it is with the truth. Those who speak the truth have always said the same thing, although according to the languages and level of understanding of their time. For this reason, it is natural that we have difficulty understanding the meanings of the past. The words were used according to the meanings they had for the people of that time.

When we talk about consciousness, we are also talking about concepts such as clarity of understanding, application, and intention. These three elements must be present for consciousness to truly occur because consciousness transcends time, language, and cultural differences. When these elements are not present, the result is the addictive state of hypnosis that people get from the religions they follow. The reason religion is designed and presented as a drug for those seeking an addiction to their dementia is precisely because of this lack of clarity.

Of course, we can't expect people with such attitudes to find clarity, let alone consciousness. And that's why religion is built around dogma, even though the problem is not so much the dogma as it is the attitude of the followers. You can't debate the speeches of Plato with someone high on heroin any more than you can reason with a follower of the Abrahamic religions.

Chapter 4: Blinded by Faith

I once met a devout follower of Hinduism on the streets of Europe. He was eager to sell me the Bhagavad Gita, a book I had read more than five times. When I told him this, he looked at me in disbelief. Even when I mentioned that I had written about it, he wouldn't listen. He was so intoxicated with his religion that he couldn't hear anyone claiming to have explained his favorite book. He told me he had been searching for answers all his life and had read many books, but he wouldn't listen when I said I had written about those answers. What's wrong with this person? He's drunk with his own illusions. He is blinded by his own certainty. The answers he seeks are not so far from him as he is from himself.

People often forget that those they want to teach may be their wisest teachers. If the answers came to him through a person passing by on the same street where he wants to sell his book, but he couldn't see it and insisted on selling me again a book I had already read many times, then there is no hope for him. I could say that this man is ignorant, but that is what lack of consciousness is - ignorance manifested by a soul in darkness. It is the mind that blinds the individual to the awareness of the obvious before his eyes. It is the same with those who have the books but cannot understand the meanings. There must be clarity for the mind to reach consciousness, and this clarity advances with time and knowledge as cultures become more complex.

For the complexity of meanings to evolve with the cultures of the world, communication must evolve in parallel. This doesn't mean that communication must become more relative, as many scholars mistakenly assume, but rather more precise and mechanical. Words are like parts of a machine that must integrate with the human mind, creating a kind of symbiosis in which the meaning projected is perfectly reflected in the mind that receives it. Therefore, such truth can only be offered by someone who can also receive a reflection from above, a being who has been enlightened and awakened by the light that has entered his mind after his personality has been shattered.

Ironically, those who are more ready to receive this truth are not those who have never been confronted with themselves, but rather those who have been forced to rebuild their personality many times through many traumatic experiences. It may not seem so to those who suffer from depression, but trauma is the precursor to enlightenment. You have to be broken before you can learn to rebuild yourself.

Although the means of communication evolve along with our understanding of the world - and we shouldn't confuse the ability to speak and listen with the ability to understand, which varies greatly from person to person - truth remains constant through time as a higher state of seeing. This seeing shows us the same today as it did thousands of years ago among the most advanced of the priesthoods. The apparent differences came in the form of interpretations, political agendas, and interference from higher forms of intelligence or extraterrestrial life that sought to manipulate humanity through the gaps that manifested in the darkness of the masses.

These gaps were found on several levels: spiritual weakness and the tendency to dull the senses through drugs of various kinds, such as alcohol; the spectrum of invisible light, which is much broader than what the eyes can see; the belief system of the masses, which is easily shaped and manipulated through the control of various segments of society. But it is in this last area that we find the most effective weapon of mass control and hypnosis, for it is indeed easier to control the masses by dividing them into different religions than by trying to get them to follow only one. It is the same principle that corporations like Nestlé, Bayer, Unilever, Johnson & Johnson, Procter & Gamble, Danone and many others use to control both pharmaceutical and food brands. The same principle is used by social networking companies to control the choices of consumers and maintain that control despite their choices.

Truth has nothing to do with faith, philosophy, opinion, or religion, but is often confused with them because greedy interests hide behind these and many other selfish manifestations of the modern world. In fact, it is not surprising that brands try to attract consumers with the same principles that religions have used for millennia, such as the promise of salvation through consumption. Take Coca-Cola, for example: The brand's classic advertising campaigns, such as "I'd like to buy the world a Coke," promote unity and harmony, much like religious messages of peace and togetherness. Apple has been known to use religious imagery and language in its marketing. Mac evangelists preach the gospel of Steve Jobs, and users are often seen as disciples. Devotion to the brand is almost religious.

As for the food and drug industries, many have been caught promoting drugs for the same diseases caused by their own foods. Nestlé, for example, has been criticized for marketing infant formula in a way that discourages breastfeeding, leading to health problems in babies, while offering "solutions" through its other products. Similarly, PepsiCo, which owns both Pepsi and Frito-Lay, has been accused of promoting unhealthy lifestyles through its sugary drinks and snacks, contributing to obesity and related health problems, while offering products such as Quaker Oats that are marketed as healthier alternatives. In the pharmaceutical sector, Johnson & Johnson has faced lawsuits alleging that its talcum powder products contain asbestos, which can cause cancer, while also producing drugs to treat cancer.

Social networking companies like Facebook use algorithms to control the information users see, creating echo chambers that reinforce existing beliefs and manipulate opinions. This is similar to how religious institutions control narratives to maintain their influence. Facebook, for example, has been criticized for allowing the spread of misinformation and divisive content that can polarize users and make them more susceptible to manipulation. But the worst mistake a person can make is to give up and say that truth is relative, and it's common for people to do that precisely because it's easier to surrender and give up than to fight so many powerful interests and the brain-dead masses.

But you can't unsee what you've seen, especially if you weren't made to be a mindless slave. When you awaken, when you become more conscious, you are able to see things that you can't unsee, unless you are willing to go back to an earlier stage of development. That is why I believe that although no religion can be accepted, all must be studied, because you can enter a stage of absolute confusion when you go through the induced mental states resulting from the mechanisms of each religion, but you also discover more transversal truths when you compare different forms of presenting the same information.

I believe that technology is helping us to reach this stage faster because the many lies of the Abrahamic religions are becoming more obvious and easier to identify. However, this technology would not be possible without the minds that created it, which means that people have become more effective at questioning themselves and what they believe to be true in their search for truth, but also more manipulated than ever. This creates the illusion of knowing a lot while knowing nothing. This is why so many people today are full of certainties about things that are absolute lies. The abundance of repeated and manipulated information creates such an illusion on a mass scale.

Meanwhile, none of the popular major language models available today allowed me to edit this manuscript precisely because it is so controversial and goes against the mainstream narrative of what people are told to believe. This means that while technology can help civilization, it will also manipulate the direction in which it goes, according to the decisions of those in power.

Chapter 5: Awakened Consciousness

We only see what we are willing to see, which means that the masses are not yet ready and able to absorb the answers to the many questions they are asking themselves. You can only increase your ability to confront and observe reality with more knowledge and experience, and you need all the knowledge you can get, because you can't increase your ability to experience unless you live faster, sleep less, and interact more with the ignorant of the world - and without letting them affect you and your inner sense of purpose, which will happen frequently as the masses are controlled by forces beyond their awareness.

The more you move forward in consciousness, the more the rest of society will try to stop you and drag you down to their level of consciousness, because that is the vibrational nature of reality on the planet. This higher consciousness that I am talking about can only be achieved naturally if we live long enough and acquire a natural determination built up from years of resilience and direct experience with the world. This is one of the reasons why so many people want to live longer. If we could live up to 500 years, many of the things I've said would be easy to see. History would be understood as it is, not as it is told, and most books would not be necessary to understand this world, because most of what is written would be considered common sense.

The purpose of knowledge leads to better thinking, and well-prepared thinking leads to higher awareness, which then helps us gain insight. However, this only happens with true knowledge, which can only be found through a proper analytical and metacognitive process of what is perceived. And since the more we can see, the less we need to know, there is a direct correlation between being enlightened, educated, aware of the nature of the world, and able to face the harsh realities of life. The secret of higher understanding remains hidden from the population because it is not in what we receive, but in our ability to process it through the mechanisms of our soul: our ability to question our own results and beliefs, and the constant practice of our analytical skills.

These skills, if they are developed at all, come late in life and in specific contexts, such as writing a dissertation. But by then the subject's mind has been so damaged by indoctrinating models that the dissertation ends up reflecting the same expectations that the system needs to maintain itself. Much of what is then taken as truth is a well-formulated lie. And because of this, anyone can reach a higher level of understanding than the best academics. In fact, some of the greatest geniuses in history did not come from the academic world.

It is through proper discernment that one distinguishes, isolates, and finds the truth, so anyone who practices these skills on a daily basis can actually attain it. The purpose of much of what the Buddha and others who were enlightened like him said was to teach us to control the mind to reach for these understandings, not to use it to escape reality. Then, through action and interaction, the one who has prepared himself to recognize and assimilate the low mental states of others can go through society without being affected by it. But by not being affected, I do not mean ignoring or isolating our thoughts or suppressing our awareness, but rather the act of going through our memories and emotions of pain faster than ordinary people in order to be able to return to our original state more quickly.

You are not supposed to suffer, and you are not supposed to deny your suffering, but you are supposed to go through it effectively and courageously, rebuilding yourself each time you are broken. We tend to admire this ability to recover and rebuild in machines and computer systems, not realizing that we are admiring what we are trying to develop in ourselves - the ability to rebuild once broken. But now that you understand this, it becomes obvious that those who say that more knowledge will make you lost are idiots and should not be heard or considered for any purpose. Many of these people are college professors, which tells you a lot about the real purpose of their job.

When someone who is supposed to be teaching you tells you that knowing too much is bad, they are trying to manipulate you or deceive you with their ignorance of their own ignorance. Many of these people are very skilled in the art of explaining their own stupidity, but this teaching has nothing to do with love, respect and freedom; it has to do with enslavement. Although the world needs more education, it has nothing to do with what is being produced in the modern education system. The kind of education people need is rarely produced by their fellow man. You will hardly find the answers you need from those who claim to have them. This is why spiritual progress, with all the knowledge it requires to be self-aware, leads us down a lonely path.

Chapter 6: Saboteurs Exposed

Whenever you find a religion that claims to want to educate you, beware, for you have found your enemy in a group of people. The worst enemies to fear are not those who threaten your life, for they are easy to identify, but those who try to gain access to your heart and soul and then poison you from within. They are present in most of the world's religions, but more so in those that attract majorities.

The masses are never attracted to religious organizations that expose them for what they are and teach responsibility and the art of self-criticism. In fact, I doubt you'll ever find one with those qualities, simply because they don't attract almost anyone. A religion that discourages masks - real or imagined - among its followers will always be among the least popular. What people really seek in religion is relief from their spiritual condition-a break from hell, not real change. So they don't change, they distort the truths they find, and end up reincarnating to do the same things they did before, with all the consequences.

A big problem with evil individuals, as I've seen, is that they get smarter. As the world evolves in its complexity and methods of communication, evil can find more alternatives to its means of control and destruction. In the face of such diversity, the majority are unprepared to deal with the attacks of the unseen world. We've only begun to identify and understand narcissists, psychopaths, and sociopaths in the last few decades, although they have always been among us. Pretty much all of our history has been made with such creatures conspiring in the dark and promoting the worst atrocities against a gullible populace.

The real demons walk among us with happy smiles and even speak on television, telling everyone what to do because people are still too stupid to see them for what they are. So it is not shocking, for example, when Bill Gates says that the solution to the problem of overpopulation is better health care and vaccinations, but it is shocking when thousands applaud and trust such madness. It would be like me saying the solution to your headache is to have a truck crush your skull, and then you applaud such an idea. That's how stupid these unevolved monkeys of human appearance are that populate the earth.

Many evil people I have personally met who are demonically possessed have become therapists and holistic doctors and have made it their life's work to pretend to help others when in fact they are destroying people in the name of helping because it's easy to fool people that way. People are too stupid to know the difference, especially when they're desperate. Many people are so ignorant that they base their judgments on their emotions and stereotypes, and then rationalize what they get based on what they have in their brains. Blinded by their ego, they can't explain their ignorance; instead, they protect it. They explain the atrocities and abuses in the world based on their good girl and good boy need for acceptance.

The masses are desperate, in need of help, a sense of belonging and comfort, and as a result, in extreme cases, go to a therapist who speaks beautiful words and further damages them. Many are beyond repair, physically, mentally and emotionally. They are too broken to be helped and that's where we get the increasing suicide statistics. This is becoming too common in my eyes, but very few seem to see the connections. You don't need to worry about magicians, witches and satanists. You need to worry, and worry a lot, about therapists and doctors who, while hiding behind helping professions, are murdering people, either by giving them the wrong medicine or by getting them to commit suicide.

I have seen it many times-doctors giving people advice that makes them die faster. It is becoming too common these days. In fact, when the coronavirus came out, we could see how many could easily lie to keep their jobs. Many doctors, nurses and virologists lied to the public about this virus and the cures because they didn't want to go against the orders they were given. Very few dared to go against the mainstream by telling the truth, and those who did were criticized, discriminated against, and in many cases lost their licenses to work and had their social media accounts deleted. Talking about one of the real cures for this virus - Ivermectin - was severely censored and punished. We were back in the dark ages of witch hunts and censorship of the truth. See how easy it was?

People today aren't very different from people in the past. In fact, they are the same. They haven't evolved enough. Killings by medical negligence, ignorance, or profit are far more common than the public is willing to accept. Many people also don't want to believe that hospitals received bonuses for diagnosing the coronavirus and putting patients on certain treatments. But this situation isn't new. Many people have been misdiagnosed with cancers they didn't have and put on chemotherapy for profit. The same goes for the many unnecessary surgeries and drugs that shouldn't be prescribed, but enrich the pharmaceutical companies and the doctors who promote them.

The path to true enlightenment and spiritual growth is fraught with hidden enemies who seek to control and manipulate. It is crucial to remain vigilant and discerning, and to question the motives of those who claim to offer help and guidance. Only through critical thinking and a deep understanding of the world can we navigate the complex landscape of spirituality and avoid the traps set by those who would prey on our vulnerabilities.

Chapter 7: Deception Unraveled

I wish I could say that it's all relative, as some people would like to believe, but it's not. Good and evil are very real, and I have seen these forces at work many times, through the least expected groups in society. But besides pretending to be invisible, another strategy used by these devils among us is to create confusion, and there's no greater confusion than that promoted by the idea of moral superiority through the distortion of historical, social, and cultural events. The truth about our history remains hidden in almost every field, no matter how advanced science is.

If the truth were known, the whole world would have to be reformulated, reorganized, and readjusted, which means that many people would lose their jobs, many books would have to be rewritten, and many others would end up in the dustbin of obsolete ideas and untruths. But when the lies are too widespread, they are more easily accepted and protected than the willingness to receive the truth. Very few souls in any period of history have been willing to receive a truth that is higher than the one promoted by their society.

For example, many people have the idea that the gods of Egypt and the God of Israel are not the same, but this assumption comes from many religious misinterpretations. Many religious books are copies of each other, and there really isn't any difference except the one based on opinion. The big difference between our religious interpretations is really only based on the opinions of those who are now skeletons, ashes, and dust.

Many of the differences and divisions in today's religions could easily be assimilated if we analyzed their descriptions with a more integrative approach. But that would also mean uniting them, which would remove the legitimacy of their separation and the claims of superiority that each of them has over other groups. In other words, if religions united, they would destroy themselves and lose their delusional followers, and that's why it doesn't happen. It is easier to murder such followers than to get them to abandon their ideologies, and this has indeed been the fate of many religious groups, including those who worship the same God.

It is interesting to note how the biblical God, for example, led groups of people who supposedly trusted and worshipped Him into a slaughterhouse, wiping out entire populations, including women and children. And for what reason? If the Jews were slaves to the Egyptians, and Moses, who claimed to be a God-inspired leader, was raised by the Egyptians, then he was raised in their religion. The leaders of both groups, collectively known as "Adonai," meaning my lords or masters-also interpreted in the Bible as Elohim, as those who came down from heaven-are not different gods or one God, but a collective presented as one.

So why would Moses promote anything other than what he had studied? He didn't! Moses "learned all the wisdom of the Egyptians" (Acts 7:20-22), and with the help of the beings collectively represented as Jehovah, Moses began to spread a new ideology to produce better slaves, an idea not directed against the Egyptian Pharaohs, but actually planned by the Egyptians themselves. The Egyptian high priest Manetho (c. 300 B.C.) states that Moses received much of his religious training under Akhnaton, the same pharaoh who pioneered monotheism.

Moses served as high priest under Amenhotep IV and was then chosen by the Hebrews as their leader. As a result, he convinced his people of the science and philosophy he had received in the Egyptian mysteries and in the way he had been instructed. In other words, the "One God" dogma he taught was the Egyptian interpretation for the New Age. The Egyptians knew and wrote that their "gods" (and not one God) traveled in "flying boats" to the heavens. They also described their gods in the early days (and before the many myths describing the gods as half man, half animal) as being of flesh and blood, with the same needs for food and shelter as humans. Homes were even built for them in Egypt, and these homes had human servants who later became Egypt's first priests.

According to noted historian James Henry Breasted, the earliest servants of the Egyptian gods were laymen who performed their duties without ceremony or ritual. Their job was simply to provide the gods with the necessities and luxuries of an Egyptian of wealth and rank at the time: plentiful food and drink, fine clothing, music, and dance. The many changes we see in Egyptian religion were related to the fact that these rulers were not well regarded by the people. The Old Kingdom (c. 2685-2180 B.C.) was followed by a period of weakness and unrest. The Great Pyramid of Cheops was broken into by unhappy Egyptians, and according to historian Ahmed Fakhry, "The Egyptians hated the builders of the pyramids so much that they threatened to enter these great tombs and destroy the mummies of the kings.

Chapter 8: Exodus Re-examined

When we consider the changes made to Egyptian religion to create the idea of an all-powerful, invisible God to inspire fear and obedience, we can question much of what is described in the Bible and the Jewish faith. Especially since, as many archaeologists have found, many of the stories told by the Jews are actually false. Dr. Zahi Hawass, former Egyptian Minister of State for Antiquitics and archaeologist, said that the Exodus from Egypt "never happened because there is no historical evidence," a conclusion also reached by Dr. Mohamed Abdel-Maqsoud, who led a team of archaeologists in search of such historical evidence.

Moreover, according to Josh Mintz, "Egyptian records make no mention of the sudden migration of what would have been nearly a quarter of the population, nor has any evidence been found of any of the expected effects of such an exodus, such as economic downturns or labor shortages. Furthermore, there is no evidence in Israel of a sudden influx of people from another culture at this time. There was no rapid departure from traditional pottery, no record or history of a population surge" (In haaretz.com). The Abrahamic religions are based on a compilation of stories created to indoctrinate a people who would easily forget the past and keep them enslaved in ignorance. Moses was trying to replicate the teachings of the Egyptians in a more effective version, instead of going against them.

We may not forget the past today because of the abundance of archaeological findings and documents that help us analyze the truth, but we choose to forget the truth in favor of our religious fantasies and then rationalize things that never happened to fit delusional beliefs, and that's why much of what humanity could know remains hidden from the public. There are too many vested interests to ensure that people are not given the facts about their true religious past, and the masses are not awakened enough to question the veracity of much of what they receive. But if Moses was a high priest of the aliens and under Akhnaton, and did not lead an exodus as historians believe, then what really happened?

The Egyptians, aware of the low level of consciousness of the masses, developed the art of hiding meanings behind symbols and structures. The Abrahamic religions produce many such hidden meanings and therefore cannot be taken as factual. The early teachings of Judaism were deeply mystical and used many hidden meanings to explain spiritual ascension, including those interpreted in the Jewish Kabbalah for those who could see, while hiding them behind folklore for those who were not ready to see, thus producing a two-tiered educational method for both the lower and higher classes. The same is true of the six-pointed Star of David, for it is a symbol with secret meanings that existed long before Judaism or King David. So if the teachings are the same and the gods are the same, then we are dealing only with perspectives, secret meanings or codes, and religious agendas.

Evidence of this can be seen in the political sphere, as when Solomon established ties between the Hebrews and Egyptians by becoming an advisor to the Egyptian Pharaoh, Shishak I, and marrying the Pharaoh's daughter. During his time in Egypt, Solomon also received instruction in the Egyptian mysteries, which is why he allowed the worship of other local gods such as Baal, the chief male god of the Canaanites. Solomon knew that the various interpretations of God all referred to the same group of beings. It is then obvious that the Jews and the Christians follow the same line of deception, that is, they follow the same division of interpretations between the fantasies for the masses and the Egyptian truths for those who can interpret them. These truths are explained by the secret mysteries of the Rosicrucians, the Freemasons, and many other organizations that work in the shadows and behind political powers, monarchies, and also revolutions and wars between nations.

Since a group needs a common enemy to justify its existence, Christians, Jews and Muslims still consider the God of the pagans and Egyptians to be Satan, not knowing that Satan - as in "the enemy" - is their own God, and that there's no difference between their religion and those they oppose. The more we believe there is an external enemy, the more we ignore the enemy within, in the form of ignorance. Fear allows this truth to be hidden from dogmatic minds. This doubt doesn't exist for Freemasons, who clearly state that their God is a combination of both God, as in Adonay - who came from Heaven - and Satan - as in the

Enemy. Freemasons have bridged the misunderstandings between Egyptian mythology and biblical fairy tales by not being afraid to accept the dual forces they represent on the chessboard floor of their temples. Albert Pike, a 33rd degree Scottish Rite Mason and author of many books on Freemasonry, explained this duality by saying, "What we must say to the masses is that we worship a God, but it is the God who is worshipped without superstition.

This God he refers to is the rebel God who liberated humanity. He explains this by saying: "The Masonic religion should be maintained in the purity of the Luciferian doctrine by all of us initiates of high degrees". Why Luciferian? Because Lucifer is the one God among many gods who delivered mankind from ignorance. As Pike explains, "If Lucifer were not God, would Adonay (the God of the Christians), whose deeds prove cruelty, perfidy and hatred of man, barbarism and abhorrence of science, would Adonay and his priests slander him?

Since Adonay is a collective of beings who tried to keep humanity ignorant, and Lucifer is the one who freed humanity from its ignorance, then the God that Christians insist on worshipping is in fact evil. This gives us a different perspective on the Garden of Eden and many other stories in the Bible as not well-intentioned, but rather designed to keep man in the dark about his spiritual nature. This is why Pike says, "Lucifer is God, and unfortunately Adonay is also God, for the eternal law is that there is no light without shadow, no beauty without ugliness, no white without black, for the absolute can only exist as two gods. Darkness is necessary for light to serve as its foil, as the pedestal is necessary for the statue, and the brake for the locomotive".

Lucifer is then, in Pike's words, the opposition to the hierarchy that has oppressed humanity, but remains as an element of our dual reality and as long as humanity continues to live in the shadows of ignorance.

Chapter 9: The Struggle of Humanity

The God of the Abrahamic religions is a God who seeks to keep humanity enslaved. It's a collective that seeks to dominate people's minds toward a common but oppressive goal. And this truth puts Moses in a new light, not as a liberator, but as a promoter of oppression, a traitor to humanity. This is indeed the case, as it is with the many prophets who followed him. As Albert Pike explains: "The true and pure philosophical religion is the belief in Lucifer, equal to Adonay, but Lucifer, God of Light and God of Good, fights for humanity against Adonay, God of Darkness and Evil" (A.C. De La Rive, In La Femme et L'enfant Dans La Franc-Maconnerie Universelle, cit. "The Question of Freemasonry", 1986).

We can now see why so many are confused by the use of these names, since the intentions of the historical figures have been distorted, many of the religious events never took place, and the true purpose of many leaders was none other than the one accepted by the masses. Moreover, when we observe that the name Satan overlaps with Lucifer, who is seen by the masses as the accuser, the deceiving spirit, and is represented by a serpent, we see that there is great confusion as to who is who in the Bible.

As Paul Anthony Wallis (former theological educator and archdeacon in the Anglican Church) explains, "In Genesis 3, the serpent is a physical being, it's one of the colonizers, and it correlates with the Sumerian character Enki, who is not a bad guy, just one who was in conflict with the chief, Enlil. The way the names are used is a little confusing, as is the way the word God is used in the Bible. But the big picture is that we are surrounded by a spectrum of beings - some physical, like ourselves, some interdimensional, some energy based, and some are nice and some are nasty, just like we have a spectrum of people on planet Earth... and the names we use may vary from culture to culture, but basically that's the big picture" (In Jeff Mara Podcast).

The conflict between Darkness and Light has always existed, not only on Earth, but also in space. It doesn't change with higher levels of consciousness and has been present between many other advanced civilizations. The battle for control of humanity is also mentioned in the Hindu texts, and some archaeological findings suggest the use of atomic bombs during this time, namely the many underground structures, artificial caverns, underground cities, and other specially constructed bunkers that seem to protect groups of people from wars with radioactive weapons.

The Sumerian tablets describe the conflict between the gods in terms of a rebellion in their hierarchy, an act of disobedience, very similar to what we find in the Bible regarding the war between the angels. But even if the biblical and Islamic interpretations explain this rebellion as originating in the refusal of Lucifer and his legion of angels to bow down to humanity, the Sumerian texts present the same event from a very different point of view. According to these texts, the first humans on Earth were unable to reproduce themselves and were later modified with the help of Enki, the master geneticist of the gods. Ancient Mesopotamian tablets credit Enki with overseeing the genetic creation of Homo sapiens. Thus, Adapa or Adam - the code name given to the first genetically engineered humans, meaning wise sons of the red planet (i.e., Mars - the place from which terrestrial humans originated) - were transformed into fully functional and independent human beings by God Ea or Enki, who was later misrepresented as the biblical Lucifer. This genetic alteration was done without the consent of Enki's brother, Enlil, and resulted in a conflict between the gods - the so-called War of the Angels in Heaven.

Enki, then the biblical Lucifer, by making humans more intelligent and able to reproduce, also made them independent and unwilling to follow the orders of Enlil and his legion. The consciousness of these humans was made superior in the process, resulting in the expulsion of the Adamic generation from Paradise - the biblical Garden of Eden. At least that is what we are told, for the most likely thing for beings awakened to their state of imprisonment and ignorance to do is to escape such a situation. These people, who were not two but many, fled paradise because it was paradise to the gods but a prison to them. This story is similar to the Mayan creation legend described in the Popol Vuh, in which the gods say: "Let us try to make obedient, respectful beings that will feed and sustain us.

In both parts of the world, the gods are described as human-like beings who descended from the heavens, and on both sides we see similarities in the descriptions presented, as well as in the pyramids. This is why when the Spanish conquistadors were met by the Mayans, they were welcomed as gods, for they did indeed look like their ancient gods, and their huge ships, never before seen by these cultures, were thought to be comparable to the spaceships their gods used to travel around the globe.

If the stories of these cultures are based on real events, there should be archaeological evidence to support them, and there is. We now know that Homo sapiens sapiens appeared on Earth abruptly, not gradually as Darwinists still insist. F. Clark Howell and T. D. White of the University of California at Berkeley said, "These people [Homo sapiens sapiens] and their initial material culture appear with apparent suddenness a little over 30,000 years ago.

Chapter 10: Sin and Salvation Redefined

Through genetic modification, humans were elevated to a god-like status, collectively known as the One God of the monotheistic religions. This allowed them to understand their previous mental state and realize that they were both naked and ignorant. Ancient Mesopotamian records show humans working naked for their masters, while the gods are fully clothed. These gods not only enslaved humans, but also maintained harems of human prostitutes, which the Bible translates as "taking them as wives" (Genesis 6:2). The Adams and Eves rightly felt humiliated, abused, and violated by their nakedness, which mirrored their situation in Eden.

The biblical Lucifer-the Sumerian Enki who delivered humanity from ignorance-became humanity's God and savior. Meanwhile, humanity's adversary, who sought to return humanity to bondage, became the enemy. Satan, the enemy of mankind, is therefore the God of the Abrahamic religions - the God of Christians, Muslims and Jews. Moses and others deceived humanity into worshipping their rulers by changing history. Humans were called sinners or descendants of Sin, a name derived from Sumerian mythology, where Sin is the son of Enlil and Ninlil. Enlil, known as the father of the gods and supreme ruler, is the biblical god opposed by Lucifer. He is both the biblical God and Satan, the enemy of mankind.

The word "sin" has been misinterpreted as the Old English "sin" or "syn," which means to miss the mark or to be imperfect. Consequently, sin has been translated as an alteration of the genetic code - an imperfection inflicted upon humanity. Original sin, attributed to disobedience and the knowledge of good and evil, is portrayed negatively, while a return to ignorance is promoted as positive. This downgrades humanity from striving to be like the gods and reduces them to slaves. This mark of the gods, or mark of the beast, can be enforced by DNA-altering vaccines, such as those forced on people in recent years under the pretext of a virus "accidentally" produced in a Wuhan laboratory with the help of certain American organizations such as the Rockefeller Institute and the Gates Foundation.

The Hebrew meaning of "sin" includes chata'ah (error), avon (distortion of God's will for personal gain), and pesha (transgression or rebellion). These terms equate sin with independent thought and refusal to obey God's will, which, according to Sumerian texts and Hebrew meanings, implies a refusal to act as a slave. Thus, according to the Hebrew texts, sinners are those who refuse to be demoted or injected with DNA-altering vaccines that destroy their cognitive abilities.

Further evidence of the application of these meanings is seen in the racial and ethnic differential impact of the Covid-19 vaccines, which were targeted to spare "Ashkenazi Jews and Chinese people," according to Robert F. Kennedy Jr. Meanwhile, the virus disproportionately harmed historically marginalized groups, with higher infection, hospitalization, and death rates among blacks, Hispanics, and Asians compared to whites (Leo Lopez, MD). Various studies have confirmed that Latinos, blacks, American Indians and Alaska Natives, and Native Hawaiians or other Pacific Islanders have the highest rates of hospitalization and death from COVID-19. Essentially, we have a virus that was created in a laboratory with the racist intent of murdering certain populations, namely Latinos, Blacks, and Native Americans. And the vaccine, while promoting a cure, is accelerating that process.

The safety of Ashkenazi Jews may be tied to their religion's alignment with this plan. Several Jewish rabbis have made statements justifying the killing of non-Jews and promoting the idea that non-Jews exist only to serve Jews. These ideas, still promoted by Orthodox Jewish leaders, emphasize that the sole purpose of non-Jews is to serve Jews. For example, Rabbi Ovadia Yosef (former Sephardi Chief Rabbi of Israel) said, "Goyim (all non-Jews) were born only to serve us. Without this, they have no place in the world - only to serve the people of Israel. (Quoted in the Israeli newspaper Maariv, October 18, 2010). Rabbi Dov Lior (Chief Rabbi of Hebron and Kiryat Arba) said: "A thousand non-Jewish lives are not worth a Jewish fingernail. (Quoted in the Israeli newspaper Haaretz, 2008).

These examples, among so many others, also lead us to understand why certain races were targeted for extermination. A study by Bond and Smith (1996) found that individuals from collectivist cultures, including some Asian cultures, were more likely to conform to group norms. In a Zionist-controlled world, Asians from communist nations would make ideal slaves, while the rest, prone to disobedience, should be eliminated to prevent disobedience among this hypothetical slave population. Thus, the offspring of the real sin of the Abrahamic religions, all of which conform to Jewish ideals, are those who accept being marked, obey a hierarchy, and follow orders - those who volunteer to be downgraded, such as those who lined up for the COVID-19 vaccines. They do not manifest a genetic flaw from the past, which was actually a change for good that made them think independently.

Today's sinners, from a spiritual and not religious perspective, are those who want to be marked by the same God who enslaved the first humans - Enlil - and who are waiting for angels to keep them in ignorance and absolute obedience, similar to a state observed in the most tyrannical nations under communist rulers, such as North Korea, China, or Cuba.

Another common misinterpretation comes from the word Nephilim, which is attributed to the sons and daughters of the gods, referred to in the Bible as fallen angels. The word has been mistakenly translated as "giants," but its true meaning is "the mighty. It refers to kings and queens chosen by these beings to control the people of Earth through slavery and war. These Nephilim never ceased to exist; their genetic background simply disappeared into the genetic pool of the masses and into the bloodlines of royal families tracing their lineage back to ancient Egypt. Thus, all of humanity has characteristics of such beings, although the Nephilim could be compared today to those who aspire to take their place, namely the Zionists and the monarchs of the world.

The Eastern Orthodox Church proclaims that original sin originated with the devil, who "sinned from the beginning" (1 John 3:8). Jehovah's Witnesses teach that every man and woman is born a sinner because of the event in Eden. The Church of Jesus Christ of Latter-day Saints blamed Adam for mankind's fallen spiritual state, adding that Adam's transgression was necessary for mankind to realize the value of what they had before. Martin Luther, John Calvin, and other Protestant reformers believed that original sin persisted even after baptism. In other words, all these and many other Christian religions that claimed to be against the misinterpretations of the original church dogmas ended up repeating the exact same teachings.

Interestingly, the Qur'an states that although there was a transgression, it was forgiven by God, suggesting that people can be forgiven for breaking free from ignorance if they willingly return to their previous state. It is a step forward in the demands for submission to the state of servitude, similar to what was done in medieval times when people were offered their lives in exchange for submission to Islamic rulers.

The true nature of sin and salvation has been obscured by centuries of misinterpretation and manipulation, but by understanding the original meanings and contexts of these concepts, we can begin to unravel the deceptions that have kept humanity in a state of ignorance and bondage. The path to true enlightenment and liberation lies in questioning the narratives we have been given and seeking the truth that lies beneath the surface. By recognizing the true nature of sin as a path to knowledge and independence, and salvation as liberation from ignorance and slavery, we can begin to reclaim our true potential as spiritual beings and co-creators of our reality. The journey to spiritual awakening involves challenging the beliefs that hold us back and keep billions in absolute darkness, far from ever evolving as spiritual beings and being liberated from this realm of bondage.

Chapter 11: Guilt Transcended

Through the many different but false interpretations of what really happened in Eden, the idea became embedded in the collective psyche that man had done something wrong and that it should not happen again in the future. Guilt, more than fear, was used to keep humanity bound to the lies of their master gods, and is still used today by the many religions as a means of keeping the masses blindly obedient. It is no accident that the original Aramaic prayer of Jesus was "deliver us from guilt" instead of "deliver us from evil" as Christians repeat today. Because evil is relative to interpretations, but guilt is very precise and easy to interpret - it is associated with being wrong for thinking independently, an indispensable trait for the development of responsibility.

One is incapable of becoming responsible, which is the quality that allows us to develop all the others related to it, such as ethics, discernment and self-analysis, whenever responsibility is replaced by guilt, or the idea that one is wrong for no other reason than not obeying certain commandments and laws. Whenever a person is trapped by guilt, he can't separate himself from his actions and analyze them. Instead, he becomes dependent on external validation, which is exactly what religions use to keep their flocks under control.

Guilt is a powerful emotion for controlling others, which is why narcissists, psychopaths, and sociopaths often use it on their victims. We have seen guilt used against people when politicians have had to find justifications for the abuses they have imposed, as when they said that those who were not vaccinated against the coronavirus were responsible for the deaths of those who were. They reinforced the idea that the sons of sin are the people of guilt and shame. But they are the ones who live in darkness and want to return to their state of bondage and ignorance.

In contrast, we have the sons of Lucifer, the awakened ones, those who seek knowledge, independence and freedom. They often presented themselves as followers of the serpent because the serpent was the symbol of Ea, not because Ea was a serpent. The Egyptians depicted their "gods" with animal heads or features to symbolize traits and personalities. Thus the serpent came to symbolize darkness - that which is occult to those who can't see, as in the occult knowledge revealed to the people of Eden.

The Sumerian tablets describe the various attempts to exterminate those who followed these values through various diseases, suggesting that these gods were constantly engaged in biological warfare. When that wasn't enough to wipe out the entire population, these gods decided to destroy the human race with a great flood. This flood was caused by a long rainstorm and the breaking of the intricate system of dams and levees that had been built in Mesopotamia to control the erratic flooding of the Tigris and Euphrates Rivers. Many archaeologists agree that there was a catastrophic flood in the Middle East thousands of years ago.

In reference to this event, the Mesopotamian Epic of Gilgamesh mentions a man named Utnapishtim (the biblical Noah) who was approached by Prince Ea, who told him that the gods were planning a flood to wipe out the human race. Ea gave Utnapishtim instructions on how to build a boat that could survive the flood, and following the instructions, Utnapishtim loaded the boat with his gold, family, and livestock, along with craftsmen and wild animals, and sailed it out to sea.

Religions contradict each other in their practice, because when one is baptized, one denies servitude to Enlil - accepts sin - and claims obedience to Enki, or Lucifer, who is the god of freedom and sexual intercourse. This is why Jesus asked to be baptized by John, since he could not be baptized in his own name if he claimed allegiance to the philosophy of Enki.

The Abrahamic religions are based on a confusion of historical events, misunderstood meanings behind rituals, and many misinterpretations - in a learning disability problem and demonstration of ignorance on a global scale - leading us to a hidden truth that is impossible to recognize by those who are not yet conscious enough to discover it for themselves. An enlightened being must necessarily reject these false doctrines because he can see that they are wrong and why. Those who cannot do this are still living under the spell of lies, in a hypnotic state, and thus trust the world presented to them to deceive them. That's why the majority, especially those who blindly follow religious doctrines, are convinced that extraterrestrials do not exist and cannot believe in such manifestations. They cannot believe because it would cause them to question all the lies they blindly follow. But only by embracing independent thought, responsibility and the pursuit of knowledge can we break free from the chains of guilt and darkness and step into the light of true understanding and freedom.

Chapter 12: Symbols Deciphered

Followers of the Abrahamic religions ridicule and reject the idea of extraterrestrial life, but have no problem believing in their own superstitions about saints and miracles, about people walking on water, or the Virgin Mary descending from heaven before them, or angels appearing before them, or Jesus having a conversation in their heads. These people are victims of their own delusions and stupidity, and as such are easily manipulated by advanced alien technology. By taking advantage of the schizophrenic state of the masses and their level of ignorance, such beings are able to transmit messages and orders that are then obeyed and carried out without any rationalization or questioning as to the intentions and purposes, just like what happened with what we call the Holy Books.

A greater deception will eventually have to come through the fulfillment of this foolishness, in which what the many religions of the world expect will be offered to them just as they want to see it - a religious war followed by angels coming down from heaven to save them. Meanwhile, there is such a disconnect between the present and the past that not many people know that their rituals are much older than they think and had different meanings. Baptism, for example, began many thousands of years earlier. The ancient Sumerians worshipped the god Enki (or Ea) in their temple in the city of Eridu with a ritual of purification by washing in the river, for Enki was also known as the god of water, magic, and incantation.

Enki was a creator who made humans slaves to the gods (on Mars) and then made them independent of those same gods (on Earth). He was also associated with semen and amniotic fluid, and thus with fertility. The cross or ankh symbol, considered a symbol of fertility and later adopted by ancient Egypt, but also by pagans and Christians, is one of the representations of Enki, Lucifer, symbolizing the union of man and woman during sex. Enki was also commonly depicted as a half-goat, half-fish creature, from which the modern astrological figure for Capricorn is derived. In Babylonian mythology, he became known as the father of Marduk, the god of water, vegetation, judgment, and magic. Later, in Greek mythology, Enlil became the Sumerian counterpart of Zeus, while Enki became the counterpart of Poseidon.

The worldwide ritual of immersion in purifying waters - common in early Mesopotamian, Egyptian, and Eastern religions, and still practiced in Hinduism, various Native American religions, and Judaism - is then a demonstration of devotion to Enki, as is the mitre - the Catholic pope's hat - a fish head representing Poseidon, Enki, and Lucifer, with its origins in Sumeria. Since Enki was also known as the Sumerian fish god, his first priests, or representatives among the people, were always dressed in fish robes. When Jesus asked to be baptized, he was performing this ritual and committing himself as a servant of Lucifer - the Light of Truth.

The era of Pisces begins with the birth of Jesus because Pisces represents Enki, and that is why Jesus is presented as the Son of God, that is, the Son of Water and Lucifer. In claiming that Jesus is the Son of God, Christians are literally saying that he is the son of Lucifer, which means that he is also a reincarnation of Marduk - the Babylonian god of judgment and magic, son of Enki. Considering that Lucifer is depicted as a goat's head, or Baphomet, and was depicted by his priests with a fish's head, and is known as the god of freedom and individualism, there's really no difference between Catholicism and other forms of Christianity, Satanism, Luciferianism, Freemasonry, Hinduism, and many other religious beliefs. They are all different aspects and interpretations of the same concepts.

Since the symbol of Lucifer - the creator of Adam - is fertility, there's also no difference between the meaning of the obelisks we find in Egypt, Washington (United States) and many other cities around the world (including Odessa, Ukraine) and the Christian cross, all of which are sexual symbols, as are the fountains in the center of many cities. The obelisk represents a large phallus or penis of Lucifer; a fountain is a symbol of Lucifer's sperm; and the Christian cross represents human procreation or sex-it is the missionary position with the man on top of the woman, made possible only by Lucifer. In other words, Christians could walk around with another sexual object, such as a penis around their neck, instead of a cross, and the meaning would be the same. These symbols of fertility represent freedom from slavery and are attributed to only one God, which is why Lucifer did not want humanity to be polytheistic.

The purpose of "his Christian son-Jesus" was to free humanity from the attempt of other religions to enslave it again. But was Jesus really the son of Lucifer, or just a representative of his faith in humanity? I think the answer is obvious, but Jesus did say, "You are gods; you are all sons of the Most High" (Psalm 82:6). Jesus also warned us of the great deception that is being manifested by using His story to do the exact opposite when He said: "Many will come in my name, saying that they represent me, and will deceive many; but you should not follow them" (Matthew 24:5). Every Christian congregation believes that Jesus was referring to some other group and that theirs is the special one, not realizing that He was actually referring to all of them.

Chapter 13: The Dawning of the New Age

The Age of Jesus, or Pisces, ended in 2020, the year in which the Apocalypse, or the Revelation of Truth, begins with the Age of Aquarius. And it is interesting to note that it was in 2020 that humanity was globally united for the first time, albeit negatively, under the same threat - fear of death by contamination. Ronald Reagan - 40th U.S. President - was right when he told the UN General Assembly in 1987: "Our global differences would disappear if we faced an extraterrestrial threat from outside this world.

This threat is attempting to correct the change of the Sumerian "genetic mistake" by genetically modifying humans again, but this time to cause everyone to lose the ability to ascend and gain consciousness of a higher realm, thus losing the potential to integrate into the 4th Density, which was brought forward with the Age of Aquarius. The Mark of the Beast, from a Sumerian perspective, is a sign of loyalty and devotion, represented in our modern world by the many governments of the planet. Because people are afraid of dying or being discriminated against by their governments and losing their basic rights, they take DNA-altering vaccines disguised as cures, which in turn blocks their potential to ascend, and then succumb to every restriction placed upon them to keep them from awakening.

This is why the Bible says, "They shall deceive the very elect" (Matthew 24:24). It is very easy to deceive the elect when they have been lost in misinterpretations for many years. But all they had to do was take advantage of what is naturally occurring. The Age of Aquarius - a symbol of water - represents the time when the Ascension promoted by Lucifer will finally be fully assimilated by the collective of humanity. It is then that humanity joins the cosmic alignment in the heavens by becoming part of the many extraterrestrial families. This happens naturally, through the awakening of one's own senses, and can only be stopped by suppressing such an opportunity, which may explain why so many governments are obsessed with preventing people from catching the sunlight.

The increased appearance of UFOs in the skies in recent years is related to these events. Humans are being given the chance to choose to ascend through consciousness, which is a great opportunity to receive more wisdom from other beings. The final battle described in the Bible is a battle between the promoters of slavery and the messengers of freedom, in which humans must choose between Enlil - representing the aliens who want to enslave humanity and merge it with AI technology, creating obedient cyborgs - and Enki - representing the aliens who want earthly humans to ascend in consciousness and join them as an intergalactic race.

This meaning as presented by the Bible has been distorted to cause humans to deny this awakening, which is naturally facilitated by a new planetary alignment in the cosmos. The Age of Aquarius is the Age of Consciousness, and can only be squandered and rejected by submission to dogma and the need for "heaven to descend to earth," rather than the opposite - the ascension of earthly humans to a position of equality with other alien races, and far from the planetary isolation they now experience. Following this interpretation, we see that what many religions are actively doing, instead of liberating humanity, is to bring it to its knees, with the help of the many governments of Earth that seek to profit from the continued enslavement of humanity, while maintaining the hierarchies that have existed for thousands of years. This is happening because as humanity awakens and sees the truth, the power of the governments and the many religions of today will cease to exist. They will be rejected as people realize the deceptions and falsehoods.

This is the meaning of the Biblical Apocalypse-the final destruction of the old world for the beginning of a new era for earthly man. Apocalypse literally means revelation-the unveiling of truth-which is the same as saying that people will no longer be kept in the dark, prisoners of the superstitions and manipulations of the powers that be. They will be liberated by the power of what has been hidden from them. Then humanity will be given the right to ascend to a higher consciousness, liberated from the situation in which it has been held for many thousands of years.

In this scenario, any prophet, such as Jesus, is inevitably a Luciferian-a follower of Lucifer's teachings and actions-who seeks to liberate humanity from its state of bondage, awaken it to its divine nature, and elevate it to the state of gods. It is precisely by saying that all men are gods and sons of the gods, as Jesus said, that the prophets of the past have opposed the hierarchy of the planet and ended up being rejected by the ignorant masses and even murdered by those in power or with religious authority. The dawn of the Age of Aquarius brings with it the potential for humanity to break free from the chains of ignorance and servitude. By embracing the truth and rejecting the false teachings that have kept us in darkness, we can ascend to a higher state of consciousness and join the cosmic alignment in the heavens.

Chapter 14: Manipulated Truth

The word Satan is the English transliteration of a Hebrew word for "adversary," but the adversary of man is Enlil, and the God of Love for mankind is Lucifer. The misuse of these two words has created misunderstandings that have led many to see enlightenment as something bad, while making the bad look good. What is occult has been associated not with enlightenment but with evil. This misidentification is so strong today that almost all knowledge of spirituality, including the Nag Hammadi library of original biblical texts, is segregated into the realm of occultism and perceived as something evil or somehow illegal.

Satan's followers, as the true enemies of humanity, are those who resist collective awakening and spiritual ascension and choose the current state of numbness that chains the masses to their masters. They can be found in any dogma that reverses the purpose of spiritual liberation, such as the dogmas of the Abrahamic faiths. But there is a choice to be made in everything we do, and we can choose freedom at any moment if we are brave enough to unchain ourselves from the emotional attachments built around other delusional people who will surely show the demons within them once we are free.

Much of this manipulation exists around the concepts of good and evil. Superstition, guilt and fear filtered through a world of manipulated meanings and concepts have blinded people to the truth. This manipulation of concepts has allowed the Sumerian system of hierarchy and religious authority over the people to continue to this day. Through various agreements and policies, those in control are able to operate in the shadows and behind the institutions that people trust. Even the power of the Pope is limited by those who control what he says and does. Those who have tested their limits have been assassinated by their own people.

For these reasons, those who are enlightened or guided by the Light are seen as those who have broken the spell cast upon humanity and can see behind the veil of lies. They are also seen by many steeped in religious superstition as demonically possessed or controlled by evil forces, because evil has become associated with denying the Hierarchy of Powers, as Lucifer did. This manipulation of meaning kept spiritual knowledge out of the hands of the masses and nearly destroyed the credibility and purpose of such knowledge, often corrupted by many who sought to use it against the people who wanted it.

Instead of places of enlightenment, many of the promises made by secret societies have turned into deeper forms of corruption and manipulation. And because the members are unaware of these things, they don't see how they are being used for evil purposes.

It is also interesting to note that the Church in general, from the Vatican to all other branches of Christianity, associates occult practices with demonic manifestations and tries to keep its members from having access to anything that promotes self-understanding or even self-development. The ignorance and fear of the masses allows for deeper control through the use of technology and information, much of it alien in nature. This is evidenced by the fact that demonically possessed people always claim to hear voices in their heads. This psychological control is no different from that which oppresses the masses through less direct methods and with means they have come to think of as their own thoughts.

Wherever you turn for salvation, you'll find the same mechanisms of control: All the Abrahamic religions tell you to obey an invisible God who speaks to you through your mind, not to question authority and its interpretation of books that often have contradictory meanings, and to be willing to be enslaved in a state of complete submission to what is seen as superior wisdom. They also condemn the acquisition of knowledge about oneself, especially if it contradicts the ideas promoted by the institutions. This often leads to exclusion from groups, which is another thing that frightens people - discrimination and segregation, or more specifically, the prospect of being alone and starting over.

The fear of being expelled from a tribe that you feel you belong to is a very old fear, because until hundreds of years ago it often meant poverty and death, because most people could not survive on their own. Today the situation is very different. People are perfectly capable of living on their own and starting a new life, even moving from one country to another with ease. But the subconscious fear that is present in our genetic structure and the memory of past reincarnations is still very much alive, and religion uses it against its followers.

When you join a group of these religious branches, you are flattered and bombarded with various forms of attention and validation so that you learn to fear losing the emotional attachments and social validation that come with it. The punishment for betraying the group mentality is the withdrawal of all this false love. Such a strategy is very similar to what individuals with Narcissistic Personality Disorder do to keep their victims attached to them. It is a tactic of mind control through one's own emotions, needs, and vulnerabilities. In fact, the favorite prey of most religions are those individuals who tend to feel isolated from society. These groups are rarely interested in people who have many acquaintances and a healthy social life because they are harder to control and manipulate. They use the exact same tactics as narcissists, psychopaths, and other human predators when looking for victims, which may explain why you find so many of these dangerous personalities in a religious congregation.

Chapter 15: Eden Revealed

The Garden of Eden is very symbolic of what causes people to obey those who would enslave them through the many Abrahamic religions, and it was a real garden on earth. "The Garden of Eden in Genesis 2 is strikingly similar to a Persian royal garden or paradise. It has an abundance of water in the rivers flowing through it, fruits and plants of every kind for food, and it is 'pleasing to the eye. God dwells there, or at least visits and converses with Adam and Eve as a king might in a royal garden" (Laura Hood, In theconversation.com). There is a reason for this similarity, for according to the Sumerian texts, the Garden of Eden (a Sumerian word for "level ground") is mentioned as being somewhere in Mesopotamia, between the Tigris and Euphrates rivers, i.e. between modern Iraq and Iran, which certainly adopted the same tradition in their own palaces. The Sumerian texts also say that Eden consisted of various Sumerian cities, each guarded by its own god, and that while humans and gods lived together, humans were servants to the gods.

The idea that there were many gods instead of just one was confusing to those who wanted to adopt a monotheistic faith, so these gods were replaced in religious scripture by angels. The meaning is the same, but the idea that there is one God rather than many gods makes it easier to control the masses, who are then subservient to a single authority rather than a multitude of superior beings with different personalities whom they can strive to surpass in intellect and knowledge. In fact, the story of Adam and Eve takes on a very different meaning if we interpret their desire to acquire the same wisdom of the gods rather than a single god. It is only natural for human beings to want to develop and become better, so it was not wrong to want to become like the gods.

According to the ancient texts, there were hundreds of gods in Eden, and these gods were not so different from humans, and they certainly passed on many customs and traditions to their servants. The Sumerian texts say that the gods had feasts, drank beer, and laughed a lot. As humans attained higher consciousness, they were able to see that these gods were not so superior or different from them, but simply more knowledgeable. Humans are then told not to worship other gods because of the rivalry between these gods and their agendas.

The Latin word "Lucifer" means "morning star" or "bringer of light," for Lucifer is the one who leads to enlightenment, a state similar to awakening, the same awakening that the sun brings in the morning. He is the one who makes humanity see. Based on this idea, many ancient civilizations learned to worship Lucifer with the sunrise, with the acquisition of knowledge, and with sex for the purpose of procreation.

Jesus confirmed that He was a follower of Luciferian teachings when He spoke of God in the following way: "His is the true light that enlightens everyone" (John 1:4, 9); and He Himself in this way: "I am the light of the world. Whoever follows me will not walk in darkness, but will have the light of life" (John 8:12) and "As long as I am in the world, I am the light of the world" (John 9:15).

Jesus was interested in uplifting humanity with an understanding of life and an ideology that he himself followed. But the biblical narrative adopts a different logic when it portrays Lucifer as the oppressor, the leader of the fallen angels or rebellious gods, but also as the devil, which means "adversary" and "opponent" of humanity. The misuse of these words in the Bible and the Qur'an is at the root of so much confusion about religion.

When man was expelled from Eden, he had to learn to survive on his own, but he was also free from his masters, which is a parallel to today's society, as few people dare to leave the system and live independently. The majority still want to follow their genetic program because they feel more comfortable working for others, enslaving themselves to those who are considered superior to them. This idea that someone who is free from the system is a rebel, an outcast, a criminal, is certainly a vivid spiritual memory that manifests today as it did then.

People still act according to their genetic program, as intended by their masters, and remain afraid to build their own lives independently and apart from the system they know. In fact, many people I meet, especially those who belong to a religion, do not see me as a prophet, but as a demon, because I possess knowledge that transcends and obliterates their dogmas. They see me as a threat and an insult to their existence, not as someone from whom they can learn. To them, I am evil because I know too much and question the validity of their lies. So nothing has changed in thousands of years of absolute nonsense, darkness and ignorance, except perhaps that people aren't burned alive in public squares for writing what billions of ignorant souls still consider blasphemy.

Religion reinforces this genetic program by keeping people obedient and confusing worshippers with words. In this way, the enemy has been able to get Christians to worship not their Savior, but their oppressor, and then to maintain the same values imposed by the oppressors of the past. Indeed, the best way to oppress someone is to keep them ignorant in the dark, for ignorance is the absence of gnosis, which is the Greek word for knowledge or information. Jesus confirmed this when he said: "The light has come into the world, but people loved the darkness more than the light. (John 3:19). Just as in His day, people today would rather remain ignorant than receive the information that would enlighten them because they are afraid to be free.

Chapter 16: Darkness Embraced

If light is knowledge, then darkness is ignorance. It follows that Christians consider the Gnostic writings to be heresy, and that the Vatican restricts public access to its library, for that is indeed the path of darkness-accepting what one is told without questioning its validity. The Vatican Secret Archives are estimated to contain 85 kilometers (53 miles) of shelves, with 35,000 volumes in the selective catalog alone.

Jesus warned us of such people when He said: "Beware of false prophets, for they come to you in sheep's clothing, but inwardly they are ferocious wolves" (Matthew 7:15); "Many will come in my name, claiming that the time is near. Do not follow them!" (Luke 21:8). Clearly, Jesus was referring to Christians and Muslims, for they are the ones who follow a book of lies while trying to convert others out of fear of end-time prophecy. They reject truth and self-knowledge while suppressing relevant information for our salvation. They are the wolves in sheep's clothing because they manipulate and distort the truth to promote lies.

The enemies of enlightenment are dogma, superstition, and ignorance, such as we find in many of today's religions. You cannot find the truth with these traits blocking your vision. The war that Christ described is a war against popular religions, and the Antichrist must be a representation of those very religions-an anti-consciousness and anti-enlightenment or anti-evolution. The Antichrist would necessarily come through these groups, and would most likely be someone who unites them, just as the Lords of Eden united themselves into one God by creating monotheism. And if such an Antichrist is a man, could he be a pope? Or is he not a man but a concept, an idea?

The deceptions of the Antichrist according to the Koran are, interestingly enough, very similar to what Jehovah's Witnesses say about the actions of their own Christian God. Both believe that people will be raised from the dead, except that for Muslims this is a trick performed by their false god. Islamic scripture says that the Dajjal (or Antichrist - whom Muslims believe to be Jewish) will say: "What do you think if I bring your father and mother back to life for you? Will you then testify that I am your Lord? You will say, 'Yes'; then two devils will take the form of his father and mother and say, 'Follow him, for he is your Lord'" (In The Islamic Antichrist by Joel Richardson). This could be a description of the act of human cloning, a feature made possible by advanced technology created on Earth or by extraterrestrials, or with the cooperation of both.

As for the possibility of Israel becoming the birthplace of the Antichrist, as Muslims believe, this is also within the realm of likely events, especially if we look at the flag of Israel and note that it contains the symbol of Moloch and has nothing to do with King David of Judaism. Moloch is mentioned by name in the Bible (in Jeremiah 32:35), where he is associated with Baal, which means "owner" or "lord" in the northwestern Semitic languages spoken in the Levant in ancient times. It then came to be applied to gods, as in the plural rather than the singular.

Moloch is also another name for Bel-Marduk, the son of Enki and the chief deity of Babylon, meaning that Marduk, as the son of Enki, the bringer of light, is reincarnated as himself, according to the teachings of Jesus. It is to Enki that Jesus refers as his father, and this makes Christianity a continuation of the Babylonian religion. We see confirmation of this in his prayer, which Christians unconsciously repeat, and which ends with "Amen," a word of Egyptian origin meaning Amun.

Amun was the Egyptian god of the occult and was depicted as a ram with curved horns. During the Middle Kingdom (c. 2055-1650 B.C.), Amun and Ra were merged as two gods in one (or the idea that the Father and the Son are one and the same). As the sun god, Ra was one of the most important and widely worshipped deities in ancient Egypt, associated with the sun, light, and growth. Ra was believed to rule the heavens, the earth, and the underworld, and he was closely associated with the pharaohs, who were seen as his representatives on earth.

The word "Amen" then appears in Hebrew and is used to express agreement, affirmation, or absolute obedience in faith. So when Christians end their prayer with Amen, they are expressing their belief in the God Amun-Ra, Father and Son, the two as one, the ruler of light, the occult, and the underworld or hell. And if Moloch and Baal are the same, and Moloch is another name for Marduk, who is also the son of Enki, whom Jesus claimed to be the son of, and Amun-Ra, as Father and Son as one, aren't all these people worshipping the same gods?

How would we distinguish the Christ as a good being if he represents Baal, the ruler of the earth? Or is the Antichrist a good deity in this scenario? It seems that either Jesus was talking about a god that is never worshiped, or he himself was representing evil powers. For if the Antichrist is the same Jesus, or Baal, Marduk, Moloch, and Amun, the prince and ruler of the earth, then we must consider that different entities were represented to hide the same level of oppression and manipulation of the masses, while adapting to the needs of the time.

It is worth noting that Moloch was an ancient Canaanite god associated with child sacrifice, Baal was the god of fertility, and Amun represents the same god. So how is Jesus, as depicted, different? This may seem confusing to those who expect the return of Jesus, for it is meant to be confusing, especially if they don't expect a being who will subjugate them and sacrifice their children. But that would be the ultimate deception: alien beings working with governments to bring about the Babylonian faith with Jesus at its center.

The Pope would not want to miss this boat, so it is in his best interest that Christianity, Islam, and Judaism unite in this global deception. But it would also be interesting to see how the many billions of sheep who worship this sun god would voluntarily enslave themselves in the name of their blind faith, culminating in a return to their origins as cognitively impaired slaves, so incredibly stupid they don't know they are naked, treated like animals, in the name of total submission to alien forces.

Another parallel with ancient religions is the fact that as the cult of Baal grew in importance, the word Baal was considered too sacred to be spoken aloud by anyone but the high priest, and the alias "Lord" was used instead. The Babylonians then used the word "Bel" (meaning Lord), and the Israelites used the word "Adonai" (my lords) for the same purpose and with the same meaning. The word Baal was eventually replaced by Yahweh in early Israelite history to signify the One who causes creation.

Chapter 17: Deception Exposed

Yahweh, Moloch, Marduk, Baal, and Jesus came to represent the same entity, which is why Jesus is presented by many groups as the Son of God and God Himself. The solar disk, called the "Aten," was a prominent symbol representing the life-giving energy of the sun and the Pharaoh's connection to divine power. This symbol is seen today in depictions of Jesus with a solar disc behind his head. However, this symbolism becomes clearer when one realizes that Jesus was presented as part of an adaptation of the same folklore, most likely invented by the Greeks based on a compilation of historical events and the need for better religious narratives.

The fact that, according to several scholars, the New Testament was probably originally written in Koine Greek, the common Greek dialect of the eastern Mediterranean during the Hellenistic and Roman periods, and then translated from that language into other languages, including Latin, Coptic, Syriac, and later Hebrew and Aramaic, rather than the other way around, is one of many clues pointing in this direction. It is estimated that the books of the New Testament were written between 50-150 A.D., so it is highly unlikely that the people of that time would have any recollection of a man performing miracles in Palestine, much less walking on water and raising the dead. Furthermore, many believe that the Library of Alexandria, from which many Greek scholars derived their knowledge, was burned by those who sought to hide the source of their newfound religion and the evidence of its falsehoods and plagiarisms.

In addition, it is worth noting that the New Testament shows influences from Hellenistic culture and philosophy, reflecting the influence of Hellenistic thought through interaction with the local communities of the time. As with many other myths of Greek polytheism, Christianity was presented as a better story to entertain the masses who, without any evidence of historical accuracy, came to believe them to be real and to worship Amun as their god. In fact, it's worth noting that the Greeks had previously copied and adapted their own religion based on the studies they acquired from Egypt and the Middle East, so it's not surprising that they would invent a more suitable folklore to entertain the gullible masses who, with the support of the Roman Empire, were looking for better teachings on morality and faith.

The Qur'an mentions that the Prophet Elijah warned against worshipping Ba'al, saying, "Do you invoke Ba'al and forsake the best of the Creators, Allah, your Lord and the Lord of your first ancestors? But this means that he was warning against worshipping Jesus. If Christians, Muslims, and Jews worship "a multitude of gods" while calling themselves monotheists, we could say that such passages, like many others, were probably invented by people who didn't know what they were talking about when they invented yet another religion full of nonsense to deliberately pit different groups against each other.

The Great Deception is a complex web of lies and manipulation designed to keep humanity in a state of ignorance and servitude. The more confusing the interpretations become, and the more the preachers try to keep people from asking questions, the more the nonsense spreads, to the point where one risks one's life simply by refusing to adhere to this nonsense. In fact, according to classical Islamic law, apostasy is considered a serious offense. Some traditional interpretations prescribe severe punishments, including death, for those who leave the faith.

This view is based on certain hadiths (sayings and actions attributed to the Prophet Muhammad) and the actions of the early Muslim community. In countries where apostasy is criminalized, penalties can range from fines and imprisonment to the death penalty. In addition to legal consequences, individuals who leave Islam may face social stigma, ostracism, or even violence from their families or communities. These social consequences can be severe and are a real concern for many people who choose to leave the faith.

This would make Islam Imbecilicity 3.0, after Christianity appeared as Imbecilicity 2.0. But the nonsense never ends, especially when we look at the modern forms of Christianity coming out of the United States. It is very likely that we are approaching the end times with a fusion of the most severe and absurd religions, which will then oppress humanity in the name of false gods.

Chapter 18: Ascension beckons

Muslims confuse their religion with Judaism and Christianity and assimilate the same principles from a new perspective because it has become another false religion full of contradictions. Divide and conquer was apparently the strategy that the gods or God used to control the population of the earth, to lead everyone into meaningless wars over who is the best servant and who can produce the best slaves. That's what the holy wars were, an attempt to prove who was most willing to be enslaved in the name of a historical lie to bring society back to its state of absolute servitude. The purpose of Islam is the same as that of any other group, which is to conquer the minds of those who have not yet been conquered and enslaved by false ideals. If you talk to members of any religious group, it is obvious that they find their religion more satisfying than any other. Thus, the divergence of beliefs under the same strategy and values keeps everyone satisfied under the same manipulative spell.

The only hope that humanity has out of this madness comes from the reincarnation of enlightened beings from other civilizations, also known as Starseeds, as well as direct contact with extraterrestrial beings through those who are ready for such interaction - those known as Contactees. The possibility of Ascension comes from these souls who speak of extraterrestrial civilizations and higher forms of consciousness. Not surprisingly, they are portrayed as crazy and ridiculed by the masses. They are also rejected by the followers of the Abrahamic religions, precisely because they can offer the knowledge that can break the spell that humanity is under, and that would naturally make people want to turn away from religious falsehoods.

On the other hand, we must not ignore those who use the subject of extraterrestrial life to do the exact opposite and, through their deception, keep humanity under the same ignorance. The tendency of some cults in recent years to portray Jesus as an extraterrestrial commander of a spaceship has certainly met the needs of those who can't get away from the lies of their groups and yet want something more and beyond these lies. Because human beings are still very limited in their ability to process information and analyze anything beyond what is known, there is a strong need to oversimplify, which keeps people from understanding higher truths. The human brain is still unable to comprehend and assimilate higher levels of complexity, such as what has been described here, when the words Lucifer, Satan, and Devil are so commonly and erroneously used.

Most people are unable to get the truth they want, even when they ask for it, and are easily deceived when they seek those answers. The answers people get are obviously more suited to their low intellectual level, and in this line Christians, Jews and Muslims have been deceived into expecting a holy war in the future to keep them united under a promise of salvation based on the old idea of "us against them". This intention to set different groups against each other is well described by Muslim apologist Osamah Abdallah, who says: "Christians believe that Jesus will come down to earth and fight for the state of Israel... What seems quite ironic to me is that the Jews, for whom Jesus is supposed to fight, don't even believe in Jesus as God or as a messenger of God..... We believe that Jesus will come down to earth at the end of the world to fight the army of Satan, which will consist mostly of the "bad" Jews, or "Zionist Jews" as we call them today, and the deceived Christians, Hindus, Buddhists, etc. .... Some will be among the "good and blessed" who will fight on the side of Jesus.

Since these religions are based on lies, another "War of the Gods" will likely show the worshipers of the gods of Eden facing a rebellion coming from heaven to stop this last attempt to enslave humanity. Although Muslims expect it to be a war between two Jesus, it is more likely to be a war between two opposing interplanetary forces for the destiny of humanity. But such a war won't happen if humanity as a whole chooses to be enslaved again and refuses to ascend to higher states of consciousness. This is why so many religions have sprung up in recent centuries, promoting the same ideologies. The intention is to make sure that spirituality is only associated with the one God, and that this God, promoted as benevolent, wise and loving, is the same one who has enslaved humanity and kept it at war all these years - the one God of the religious books.

In this way, the masters who have enslaved humanity are able to maintain their power over humanity, which will then refuse to be saved by those who truly have such a purpose. We are already seeing this with many religious scholars and priests claiming that aliens are demonic spirits, as well as attempts to merge man and machine, creating a civilization of cyborgs through the use of nanotechnology - already present in many vaccines.

Chapter 19:
Civilization Chipped

The advent of microchipping and nanotechnology promises to create more compliant subjects than those of ancient times, as these individuals can be easily monitored and controlled. This phenomenon is not new; throughout history, false prophets have sold their people into monotheistic ideologies, claiming to help humanity while actually enslaving them. Today, these false prophets are scientists and health experts who, under the guise of progress, are leading humanity into a deeper spell from which it may never recover.

Jesus warned of this struggle when he said, "Send forth your light and your truth; let them lead me" (Psalm 43:3). He was not positioning himself as a leader, but rather emphasizing that truth and light would guide those who sought a higher truth. Notice that he combines light and truth and places himself at the end of these values, unlike religious scholars who place Jesus at the center of their dogmas. According to Jesus, "the nations that are saved will walk in his light" (Revelation 21:24), meaning that these nations will choose love and truth over religious dogma. What nations love truth and reject dogma? Could he be referring to the forgotten islands in the Pacific Ocean that the Vatican had no interest in evangelizing and the British and French overlooked, or those where preachers are still greeted with arrows?

The hope of salvation lies in moving to a land without dogma or superstition, but finding such a place is difficult, since almost the entire planet has been colonized with lies and superstitions. In this context, Luciferianism is not a religion of evil, but of enlightenment, since the real evil lies in religious dogma, especially that of Christianity and other Abrahamic religions. Christianity was so corrupted that even bishops disagreed on basic beliefs. One such belief was the birth and identity of Jesus. For example, Arius, a presbyter and priest from Alexandria, Egypt, proposed that Christ was not divine but a created being. Arianism held that God was a unique being and that Jesus was merely a man, not the incarnate God. They rejected the mainstream Christian doctrine of the Trinity.

Arius' opponents, including Bishop Athanasius, argued that Arius' teaching reduced the Son to a demigod and undermined the Christian concept of salvation. Among the opponents of Arianism was Bishop Lucifer Calaritanus, who founded the Luciferians-an orthodox Christian group that sought to perpetuate his rigorously orthodox views. These Luciferians and other Nicene Christians won the debate, leading to the rejection of Arianism. Emperor Constantine ordered the death penalty for those who refused to renounce Arian writings and condemned them as heretics. This Luciferian doctrine, dominant in many modern Christian congregations, tells us that Christ and God are both the same and different, meaning that when Christ prayed, he was essentially talking to himself, even though they were two different entities. This concept is perplexing and raises questions about the coherence of Christian beliefs.

We could assume that Lucifer and Jesus are father and son and the same if Jesus were a clone of Lucifer, but that would require acknowledging the existence of Lucifer and a cloning process. Meanwhile, various Christian sects are shocked to hear priests in the Vatican chanting in Latin: "Oh, Lucifer, who will never be defeated, Christ is your son. Yet this phrase is consistent with Christian beliefs, since the Luciferians won the debate and declared Jesus to be the Son of God-Lucifer and Lucifer as well. Everything else we see in various Christian denominations is just different branches of the same rooted nonsense. This widespread nonsense suggests that if you believe in Jesus as the Son of God, you also believe that the miracles of the Holy Church are performed in the name of Lucifer, and that the Luciferians represent the true branch of Christianity.

Isn't it ironic that the Inquisition tortured and burned thousands of people based on the same premise? It seems that the Holy Church is not very different from opportunistic sociopaths and narcissists who try to hide their evil by finding scapegoats to falsely accuse, publicly humiliate, and then sadistically punish. Why, then, should Christians have trouble accepting that the Vatican is involved in child abuse and perhaps ritual sacrifice in hidden chambers? Aren't these practices consistent with the faith? Perhaps they are more consistent than many Christians dare to believe. In fact, many scholars believe that the biblical Jesus was arrested not because of his faith, but because he was a pedophile who engaged in ritualistic practices with children. This is suggested in the Gospel of Mark (14:51-52), which states that Jesus was arrested in the Garden of Gethsemane after being found with "a young man wearing nothing but a linen garment" who "fled naked, leaving his garment behind" after Jesus' arrest.

The Greek word translated "young man" is neaniskos, which was associated with teenagers. This puts Jesus in a similar light to the Prophet Muhammad, who married a six-year-old girl named Aisha. But how far have we come since then? In Iran, the legal age of marriage for girls is 13; in Pakistan and Indonesia, 16; and in Afghanistan, more than 35% of girls are married before the age of 18, often as young as 9 or 10. This is often done with the consent of the family, who sell their daughters against their will to the highest bidder. This is religion legitimizing and legalizing pedophilia and rape.

As for the crimes of Christianity, according to a 2004 report by the John Jay College of Criminal Justice, commissioned by the U.S. Conference of Catholic Bishops, some 4,392 priests were accused of sexual abuse between 1950 and 2002, but only 10% were prosecuted and sentenced to prison. In Australia, according to the Royal Commission into Institutional Responses to Child Sexual Abuse, 1,880 priests working between 1950 and 2010 were accused of child sexual abuse, but less than 10% were prosecuted and sentenced to prison.

Chapter 20: Secrets Exposed

The ITCCS-International Tribunal into Crimes of Church and State-founded in 2010 by Nobel Prize nominee Reverend Kevin Annett to unite survivors of genocide and child torture across borders and to build a broad political, spiritual and legal movement to dismantle the Vatican and other churches and governments responsible for historic and ongoing crimes against children and humanity, found evidence presented at the Brussels Common Law Court that more than 50,000 missing children are allegedly suspected victims of an international child sacrifice cult known as the Ninth Circle. A Catholic Jesuit Order document entitled "Magisterial Privilege" (dated December 1967) was presented to the court by the chief prosecutor, showing that each new pope was required to participate in the Ninth Circle's satanic ritual sacrifices of newborn children, including drinking their blood.

"Documents from the Vatican's secret archives presented to the court also clearly show that for centuries the Jesuits had a premeditated plan to ritually murder kidnapped newborn babies and then consume their blood," the chief prosecutor told the five international judges and 27 jurors. The plan was born out of a twisted notion of deriving spiritual power from the lifeblood of the innocent, thereby ensuring the political stability of the papacy in Rome. These acts are not only genocidal, but systemic and institutionalized in nature. "Since at least 1773, they seem to have been carried out by the Roman Catholic Church, the Jesuits, and every pope" (In Christianobserver.net). But it is all in keeping with their belief system, for if Christ is the son of Lucifer, then Christ is Moloch, Baal, and Bel-Marduk, the deity to whom the Babylonians offered child sacrifices.

The religious miter worn by the Pope and his bishops represents a fish's head in honor of Enki, the Sumerian god of water, creation, and knowledge, also known as Lucifer in the modern interpretation of this story. The misuse of words is abundant and naturally confusing, as when we use the word God to represent the opposite of dog, which implies the opposite of a loving, loyal, and compassionate creature, to characterize a brutal, tyrannical ruler. This is no mere coincidence, considering that in the cult of the Bohemian Grove, politicians and other famous personalities are called to practice the "cremation of care" in front of a giant 12-meter owl, which represents Moloch.

Notable personalities who have participated in this madness over the years, in which members are naked, wearing only white and black robes, worship an owl, and spend a few days surrounded by prostitutes, include (in alphabetical order) Ambrose Bierce, Art Linkletter, Bret Harte, Calvin Coolidge, Charlie Chaplin, Charles Schwab, Clint Eastwood, Colin Powell, Douglas Fairbanks, Dwight Eisenhower, Frank Borman, George Bush Sr., George

Schultz, Gerald Ford, Henry Kissinger, Herbert Hoover, Jack London, Mark Twain, Pete Wilson, Richard Nixon, Ronald Reagan, Wally Schirra, Walter Cronkite, Will Rogers, and William Howard Taft. Even Britain's Queen Elizabeth was seen there in 1983. "Her Majesty was honored with an ecstatic pagan dance ceremony, complete with expensive, elaborate stage props such as Egyptian pyramids and Babylonian ziggurats" (In Money for Power by John P. Hunter III).

The purpose of worshipping this owl, in a ritual they call the "cremation of care"-in which one abandons one's feelings of compassion, empathy, and love for human life-is not the only thing going on. "Stories have come out of the Grove of wild homosexual orgies, male and female prostitutes engaged in what can only be described as extreme sexual play, young children being exploited in unspeakable ways up to and including cold-blooded ritual murder. There are stories of actual human sacrifice on the 'altar' of the Owl God statue" (In Secret Societies by Nick Redfern).

Understandably, it's all very hard to believe until reporter Alex Jones managed to infiltrate the site and record the actual event taking place. In essence, leaders from around the world and in various positions of power are showing their allegiance to the gods by practicing rituals that demonstrate the abandonment of empathy, because only a psychopathic drive for power and against humanity can justify keeping such figures in places of influence. So we can say that there is no difference between the assumptions made about Moloch, God, and pure evil. And while we can debate whether Jesus represents good or evil, there is no doubt that many lies and abuses are perpetrated in his name while keeping the masses docile and obedient to those who worship giant owls and engage in massive sex parties.

Chapter 21: Power and Faith

Have Christians been deceived into worshipping Moloch disguised as a mythological figure named Jesus who never existed? Is there a conflict of faith when famous public figures claim to be Christians and then are accused of child sacrifice and witchcraft?

In ancient Babylon, people worshiped Moloch by sacrificing children to him, just as former U.S. Secretary of State Hillary Clinton allegedly referred to in a 2009 email to former U.S. adviser to President Barack Obama, John Podesta, as revealed by Wikileaks. The Clinton-Podesta email scandal is full of references to both pedophilia and Satanism, such as "spirit cooking" and "sacrificing a chicken," which many claim is a code word for children. Psalm 106:34-43 says of the Babylonians, "They sacrificed their sons and daughters to demons, shedding innocent blood, the blood of their own sons and daughters, whom they sacrificed to the idols of Canaan, defiling the land with bloodshed."

Evidence that the world's elites are involved in child sacrifice was also presented by Ted Gunderson, former director of the

FBI. He claimed that there is an international child trafficking and pedophilia ring associated with various rituals. These include selling children into slavery and flying them to Washington DC to be used in sex orgies by politicians. With more than 100,000 children missing each year in the U.S., Gunderson stated that the FBI is fully complicit in the cover-up. Not surprisingly, the Hillary Clinton case has been forgotten. According to former FBI Assistant Director James Kallstrom, Bill and Hillary Clinton are part of a "crime family" that has created a cartel to bribe and intimidate top officials whenever one of their crimes is under investigation. He also said that Hillary Clinton is a "pathological liar" and predatory sexual offender, and Bill Clinton is a serial rapist whose crimes have been covered up by successive generations of corrupt officials on the Clinton payroll (in an interview with John Catsimatidis).

Footage found on the laptop of Anthony Weiner (Huma Abedin's husband, who was jailed in 2017 for sexting with a minor) is said to have caused some of the most hardened NYPD officers to cry, vomit, and seek psychological help. Sources claim the footage shows Hillary Clinton and Huma Abedin raping, mutilating, and terrorizing a prepubescent girl, deliberately causing the child's body to release adrenochrome into her bloodstream before bleeding her out and drinking the blood in a satanic ritual sacrifice. According to those familiar with the elite's drug of choice, drinking such blood produces an "intense" and "exotic" high.

Part of a blood sacrifice or not, the trend of drinking blood is growing worldwide and becoming big business. "Communities of ordinary people - nurses, bar staff, secretaries - regularly drink human blood" (BBC.com). According to Dame Linda Partridge, a geneticist at University College London, "research shows that young blood could allow people to live free of diseases such as cancer and heart disease until they die" (The Times). Researchers at the startup Ambrosia saw improvements in biomarkers for several diseases after 70 participants in a study were given plasma-the main component of blood-from volunteers aged 16 to 25. Another startup, called Elevian, announced it had received a $5.5 million investment to back its approach. Ambrosia currently offers teen blood plasma to older customers at a cost of $8,000 for two and a half liters. Could it be, then, that religions are nothing more than organizations invented to hide the perversions of the world that have never ceased to exist?

Furthermore, why is the name Jesus still used by so many religions when there's no secular evidence from the first century to support the existence of anyone named Yeshua Ben Yosef? The period in which Jesus Christ is said to have existed is one of the most documented periods in ancient history, yet there is virtually no historical evidence of his supposed existence in any contemporary historical record, which would certainly not go unnoticed if he performed so many miracles.

Bart Ehrman, professor of religious studies at the University of North Carolina at Chapel Hill and Rutgers University, said, "Strange as it may seem, there is no mention of Jesus by any of his pagan contemporaries. There are no birth records, no trial transcripts, no death certificates; there are no expressions of interest, no heated slanders, no passing references-nothing. In fact, if we extend our field of concern to the years after his death-even if we include the entire first century of the common era-there is not a single reference to Jesus in any non-Christian, non-Jewish source of any kind." Ehrman adds, "We do have a large number of documents from the period-the writings of poets, philosophers, historians, scientists, and government officials, for example, not to mention the large collection of surviving inscriptions on stone and private letters and legal documents on papyrus. In none of this vast array of surviving writings is the name of Jesus even mentioned.

Alex Collier explained, "Constantine was so busy burning the resources of the Roman Empire and stopping the religious wars that he decided to create a state religion. He then took the religions of the West, which worshipped Isis, and the religions of the East, which worshipped Krishna, and put them together-the 'Isos-Kristos' we know today as Jesus Christ" (In Defense of Sacred Ground).

Chapter 22: The Trinity Debunked

The fundamental problem faced by the Council of Nicaea is that once you separate Christ from God, you label Him as just another prophet, as the Islamic faith claims, and thus risk the disappearance of the Christian Church. This separation also distances Christianity from its Sumerian and Babylonian roots, giving more importance to the teachings of the early Gnostics and allowing more controversy from the religious groups they sought to suppress. In addition, by claiming that God is one, but not the same as Jesus, the values of Christian doctrine become relative to the interpretations of each rival group.

According to Everett Ferguson, "The great majority of Christians had no clear views on the nature of the Trinity, and they did not understand what was at stake in the questions surrounding it" (In Church History, volume one). Although the Proto-Orthodox won the earlier disputes, they were declared heretics not because they fought against ideas considered theologically correct, but because their positions lacked the precision and refinement required by the fusion of several contradictory propositions accepted simultaneously by later Orthodox theologians. Bart

Ehrman argues that this is why the Trinity is such an absurd, irrational concept, and yet necessary. If this makes any sense, the idea of a Trinity had to be accepted in order to find agreement among disagreements.

The final decision had more to do with the survival of the Christian Church than with logic, and the Luciferians ended up justifying their name with the belief that Christ was the representation of Moloch on earth, and that the ascent to Lucifer could only be made through Christ. And while this doesn't mean that Christians are evil for worshipping Moloch through the figure of Jesus and sex symbols through the use of the cross, many of them, and almost every one I've ever met, are indeed very evil. It is hard not to be influenced by an evil deception when you willingly participate in it. It would be like saying that there are compassionate people in the army who don't want to murder anyone.

The reason Christianity embraces the evil predispositions of its members is explained by the dogmas of its belief system and the way it is constructed, for only those who don't dare question and are willing participants in a cult of obedience and childlike figures would be attracted to an ideology that perpetuates such attitudes, attitudes of the same low vibrational nature. These low vibrational individuals are equally and easily manipulated through their fear based predisposition with little or no explanation of the demands presented. It is a childish mentality where the ideas of a God presented as a father figure fit well with the cognitive impairment of his followers.

Whenever one descends into the vibration of fear - fear of not being accepted by a Christian community, fear of what others think, fear of not going to heaven, fear of not being chosen in a supposed rapture to heaven, and so on - he ceases to be a co-creator, a sparkle of the light of creation, and becomes a creature of darkness - subject to apathy and a passive role in the events unfolding before him. He becomes a volunteer in his enslavement and spiritual decline. When this happens, when one expects to be saved by some mysterious external force that manipulates and lowers his cognitive potential, he has given up consciousness, responsibility and spiritual creativity, which are the exact opposite vibrations manifested in a human being.

Such an individual descends to the lowest vibration, which is apathy, the closest thing to death, which is why so many Christians seem to desire it, often above the desire to do good for others. Those who live in fear and terror are easily manipulated because their thoughts are based on survival and instinct. They are focused on their own needs. Their reptilian brain is constantly stimulated, which is why so many religious people seem to be racist and hostile to other faiths. They are driven by the part of the brain that tells them that their lives are in danger, that there are opposing forces against them, and that their existence is more important than that of others.

This mindset is what led Europeans to fight Muslims in the Middle Ages, and then led them to believe that anyone who is not a Christian is a threat, thus justifying the mass genocide of many tribes in South and North America. It also led to the many misrepresentations of Buddhists and Hindus as devil worshipers and a lack of empathy for members of these religious groups. Most Christians are so caught up in the vibration of fear that they even see aliens as demonic spirits descending from the sky and their shape-shifting technology as proof of this, making them not so different from the witch hunters of centuries past who saw the reading of any book that wasn't the Bible as a practice of devil worship.

What I am trying to say here is that their religion is not what they think it is or claim it to be, nor has it ever been. The most evil people, the biggest liars and slanderers, the most psychologically abusive and uncivilized, and the most offensive people I have ever met in my entire life have all been Christians of various denominations and faiths. Their level of resentment and hatred, hidden behind a facade of false friendship, is beyond human understanding. But they seem confused and in need of therapy because they do not represent anything resembling compassion for others. They believe that compassion is conditional on the dogma they espouse and is only deserved by those within the same congregation.

The dogmas Christians follow don't make them better, they make them more self-entitled, narcissistic, and selfish. And there is no greater demonstration of what I just said than when you hear people in speeches at protests in Poland claiming that they don't want Arabs in their country because they are a Christian nation. These Polish Christians seem to be too stupid to realize that their Jesus was also an Arab. He wouldn't be welcome in this country that portrays him as a white man with blond hair, and where the locals look down with contempt on anyone who is not white-skinned.

Poland is one of the many examples of what religious misinterpretation and stupidity can do to an entire nation that should disappear for a better future for the people of the world. Furthermore, they should not be allowed to continue to promote divisions based on a delusional idea of racial supremacy in a continuation of what they did during the Nazi occupation. But the average European and American Christian today would not be willing to sit next to someone of Palestinian appearance, someone who probably resembles the Jesus they claim to follow.

Modern Christianity is as full of racists as it is full of absolute stupidity, and yet many religious people I have met from the US and European nations claim to be Christian while being extremely racist. It makes absolutely no sense. But racism can be so obvious that Christians do not even try to hide it, like when I entered a cathedral in London with a white and blonde girl by my side and they immediately tried to talk to her and recruit her while completely ignoring me as I stood by her side. I have seen this kind of behavior many times. You can't be a Christian and a racist unless you are psychotic, hypocritical, and incredibly stupid. These three words accurately classify modern Christians.

Chapter 23: Christianity Unmasked

The most devout Christians are often very evil individuals because Christianity, as it is often practiced, promotes division and distrust between Christians and other members of society. It builds cults and closed communities around the idea of moral superiority and incites subliminal messages of hatred against non-Christians and non-whites, especially in communities where Christ is portrayed as a symbol of white supremacy rather than as a Palestinian man, which is his most likely appearance.

I have been in dozens of different Christian groups for several decades and can say without a doubt that Christians are some of the most evil people I have ever met. Their evil is not always visible to others; it comes from contempt for differing viewpoints, resentment of those who ask them questions they can't answer, racist views of others, and toxic behavior associated with their dogmas and interpretations of the Bible. In particular, their views on the end times and the glee they take in describing the deaths of other people for their ascension is disturbing and instills in them a sense of delusional superiority similar to what we see in individuals with narcissistic personality disorder.

As for the return of the God-Lucifer of the Judeo-Christian religions that many are waiting for, I have bad news for them: God is dead. According to Sumerian stories, Enki, or Lucifer, was murdered by his brother Enlil. His tomb is on Mars. Enki will not return to save humanity. If he does, it will be a staged event designed to deceive humanity into complete servitude. Unless, of course, we are dealing with the return of his reincarnation, which is the most likely link between modern and ancient beliefs. This would indeed make sense, but the problem is that modern Christians don't believe in reincarnation. They have constructed a much more illogical story than the ancients, who at least had more ways to rationalize themselves.

As William Bramley explains in "Gods of Eden," "Mankind appears to be a slave race languishing on an isolated planet in a small galaxy. As such, the human race was once a source of labor for an extraterrestrial civilization and remains a possession today. In order to maintain control over its possession and to keep Earth as a kind of prison, this other civilization has bred never-ending conflicts among human beings, promoted the spiritual decay of human beings, and created conditions of unrelenting physical hardship on Earth. This situation has existed for thousands of years and continues to this day.

After the death of Lucifer, the Gods sought to eliminate rivalries among themselves and return humanity to its former state of servitude. This had to be done through Lucifer's representatives, so they introduced monotheism and various religions to confuse the masses. In order for this plan to succeed, the rituals dedicated to Lucifer, which were supposed to represent freedom from oppression, were collectively reinterpreted as a way of proving subservience to the gods. Thus, baptism, instead of being a ritual of spiritual liberation dedicated to Lucifer, became a ritual of enslavement and servitude to the gods. The symbols of Lucifer were also separated from their true meaning and are now associated with evil, namely the symbol of the serpent.

Lucifer was not only a scientist, but also a priest-god, often depicted as a serpent because that is the symbol of spiritual ascension. The snake was the symbol of his religion and is still associated in India today with kundalini energy - the rise of our life energy through the chakras of the body. This information was suppressed, and everything that represented the snake was made to be hated and feared - as in the biblical meaning attributed in the allegory of God's reaction to the animal. What had once been a religion of enlightenment was corrupted by a religion of dogma, superstition, and apocalyptic fear. Humanity was thus deceived into fearing the very teachings that led to enlightenment. And by calling themselves one, the gods were able to replace the previous worship of the one-god Lucifer.

Since then, the true teachings of the Spirit have been corrupted or simply hidden. This has been the case with every single new group that has attempted to educate humanity in the hidden mysteries, including those that claim to be branches of the Egyptian Enlightenment. Satanism, too, as an opposition to the idea of slavery and ignorance promoted by the biblical teachings, instead of being a religion of love, became a religion of hate, falling prey to the tricks of the Christian faith. Buddhism, in its essence, for a long time preserved the original teachings of attaining Nirvana through a practice that makes one more conscious, but today is the exact opposite and many Buddhists are convinced that the purpose of Buddhism is to have no thoughts and to become as nothing, detached from everything.

Although we can argue whether Christ really existed or was merely a Greek invention, there is no doubt that the Gnostic teachings associated with this figure sought to enlighten and liberate humanity from ignorance, with teachings parallel to those of Buddha. For this reason, many Buddhists thought he might be the second Buddha, meant to give a sequence to the original teachings, since the message of love and self-reliance was the same, and both spoke of a creative force in the universe. But these teachings have been lost for nearly two thousand years, and once found, have been completely ignored by those who claim to follow Christianity. Modern Christians follow dogma and don't care about the truth, especially if it contradicts their dogma rather than reinforces it.

Since there is no such thing as good and evil, but a process of ascension in which most of humanity is at the bottom, humanity has been kept in the dark about its nature and potential by the Abrahamic religions. The nonsense propagated by these groups functions as a puppet show that promotes division, resentment, duality and antagonism, and is run by the same puppeteers who have been playing both roles in this show for thousands of years. By playing with a polarity between extreme fear and absolute obedience, such a group is able to maintain control over the gullible and extremely ignorant and primitive masses who beg to be enslaved in a complete subservient attitude to those they think are their saviors.

Chapter 24: Abraham Deceived

It is easy for outside forces to deceive people because the Abrahamic religions are nothing more than a theater of foolishness. All they have to do is convince people that they are interacting with God, demons, or angels, and play some holographic images that represent what such individuals have in their minds. It wouldn't be difficult to assume that someone could travel back in time, show a hologram appearing as an angel to an ancient man, and make him believe anything. However, the ancient writings, contrary to modern beliefs, do not hide the fact that such angels were visitors from other planets, not always with the best intentions towards humanity.

Based on these facts, we could ask ourselves whether the Vatican is responsible for both inviting evil forces and training exorcists to fight them, just as the CIA and Mossad train terrorist organizations with the intention of overthrowing the regimes they do not want in power, and then send their troops to fight such groups when such organizations are deemed uncooperative. Several investigations, most notably those uncovered by reporter Gary Webb, have also proven that the CIA supplies drug dealers in major U.S. cities and uses drug money to finance illegal operations while slowly murdering the country's undesirable underclass.

This cat-and-mouse game keeps the masses distracted with their own need to survive, divided, frightened, and most of all, obedient. When this isn't enough to keep the masses obedient and under control, the CIA drugs and hypnotizes criminals through various projects, namely MK-Ultra, to do exactly what the CIA is sworn to protect people from - mass shootings. Because there is nothing like a general panic to keep people at home and distracted from dealing with more important issues.

Illusionists like Derren Brown have shown how easy it is to pick a random person off the street and then hypnotize them into believing anything, even a simple arcade game. As many illusionists have proven, the vast majority of the population is susceptible to hypnosis and will believe anything you tell them. These tactics are similar to those used throughout history to create many of the supposed messiahs and prophets. Muhammad, for example, was either semi-conscious or in a trance when the angel Gabriel commanded him to "Recite!" and record the message the angel was about to give him. The angel's command to Muhammad was similar to the commands given earlier in history to Ezekiel of the Old Testament and to "John" of the Book of Revelation. When Muhammad awoke, it seemed to him that the angel's words were "written on his heart," indicating that he had been drugged and psychologically implanted with the messages he was to pass on to others.

Mohammed's mission was to create a new religion called "Islam," which means "surrender"-a step forward in the monotheistic idea of obeying the "one God. Thus, followers of Islam must "submit" to God, and since members of Mohammed's faith are called "Muslims," meaning those who submit, they form another group of blind and ignorant obedient sheep. Mohammed also said that "Allah" is the same God as the Jewish and Christian Jehovah, so the intent to create another group of slaves to set people against each other was clear. These gods deliberately created different monotheistic religions to keep people constantly at war and to strengthen their faith in their chosen religion of enslavement.

The Abrahamic religions all have the same purpose, and monotheism, at least as presented by these religions, is designed to keep people at war in the name of lies. This is evidenced by the Hebrew names of God - Adonai and Elohim - both of which are plural, not singular, as is the word Jehovah, which comes from the word Adonai, and the word Allah, which stands for Jehovah.

Paul Anthony Wallis explains that "if every time we find the word Elohim, we translate it in its root meaning, instead of what the translators are currently doing, where in one text it's God and in the next it's the devil, in one it's demons and in one it's false gods, in one it's landlord chieftain or chieftains, and even angel or angels,... What if we take a step back from these arbitrary choices - because they are arbitrary, it's just according to what's happening in the action that determines which of these words gets picked,... what if we just use the root meaning,... how do the stories change? The moment you do that, the stories obviously change, but they don't change in a random way, the way they change is that they flip in such a way that they parallel the ancient Sumerian, Babylonian, Arcadian, Assyrian stories and the ancestral stories of cultures all over the world. Suddenly it's clear that the biblical stories of the mighty are a retelling of the Sumerian stories of the celestial people, or the Mayan stories of those who made man? They're not stories about God. God isn't really mentioned in these stories. These stories are the memory of this ancient culture of contact between our ancestors and extraterrestrial visitors who came from another planet, colonized planet Earth, and genetically engineered our ancestors to be, in effect, a labor force for them. That's the story hidden in the Bible. You make this one change in the translation and the story stares you in the face" (In Jeff Mara Podcast).

Chapter 25: Aliens and Origins

Christians unwittingly follow an alien religion and worship the dual forces manifested by these entities. They seek and avoid the same energies as if good and evil were merely different emotional expressions of these entities. As Paul Anthony Wallis explains, "The moment you have two entities arguing about how intelligent human beings should be, and the entity translated as God wants human beings so unintelligent they don't even know they're naked, that's how interested the God character is in human progress... The moment you do the translation work, you realize that this isn't the story of God and the Devil going at it, it's the story of the Powers That Be arguing among themselves about how intelligent they want human beings to be; and there's one person, one faction that breaks ranks and says 'we're going to do an upgrade, we're going to take them from all-male to male-female, we're going to take them from sterile to fertile, we're going to take them from unintelligent to intelligent'; and after the upgrade is affected, well, there's a huge stink and conflict over it" (In Jeff Mara Podcast).

This narrative echoes stories found in Sumerian, Greek, Norse, and Mesoamerican texts. These parallel stories are told throughout the world. If there is any doubt that the Abrahamic God is a multitude of extraterrestrial beings, Ezekiel's descriptions can dispel it. Ezekiel tells us: "I saw visions of God. And I looked, and behold, a whirlwind came out of the north, a great cloud, and fire flashed, and there was brightness about it, and out of the midst of it shone something like a pale yellow metal. And out of the midst of it came four living creatures. And this was their appearance: they had the likeness of men. And their feet were straight feet, and the sole of their feet was like the sole of a calf's foot; and they shone like burnished brass. And they had human hands under their four-sided wings. Their wings were joined together, and they did not turn when they walked, but they all walked straight. As for the appearance of their faces, they had the face of a man, and the face of a lion on the right side, and the face of an ox on the left side, and the face of an eagle. And when they went forth, I heard the sound of their wings, like the sound of many waters, like the voice of the Almighty, like the sound of an army. When they came to rest, they lowered their wings. And there was a voice from the crystal cover that was over their heads as they rose and lowered their wings" (1:1-25). The voice told Ezekiel that it was "the Lord his God" (Ezekiel 2:4).

Ezekiel describes the Abrahamic God as many represented as one, not symbolic or angelic, but real beings with human appearances. He notes that they are not as mysterious as religion makes them out to be. The "great cloud" in which they traveled was clearly made of "metal," he says. The creatures looked like ordinary people, or "in the likeness of men," and they probably wore boots, as he uses the term "calf-foot" in comparison to his sandals. He had never seen such boots before. He also mentions that they had "human hands" and that they traveled in a vehicle with "four-sided wings," similar to a modern drone. These descriptions were of a vehicle that, in the simplicity of Ezekiel's understanding, was part of God Himself. Ezekiel, like many before him, lumps everything into the word "God" in his description, including vehicles, spacecraft, and the aliens, even though he clearly distinguishes the beings as looking human. Ezekiel's description is consistent with others in the Bible who suggest that Jehovah, Elohim, God, or whatever we call Him, refers to ET beings of human appearance flying in spaceships.

The temperament of these gods is also similar to that of humans, for they are happy only with absolute servitude and become angry with disobedience. They order the genocide of entire populations that do not obey them, thus bringing civilization to its current state, dominated by humans under their control and the control of their priesthood. This clearly shows that they have no interest in the liberation or spiritual ascension of humanity. In fact, this group is so incredibly psychopathic, narcissistic, and cruel that it has led some to wonder if they are really from an advanced civilization or rather from our own future. There is certainly no reason to worship them and build religions around blind obedience to their teachings, which are obviously false and designed to keep humanity in the dark and obedient.

The religions these beings promote to their prophets seem to be constant updates of their intention to keep humanity ignorant, while also using these new groups to exterminate previous ones deemed undesirable. This is why the Christians persecuted the Jews and other Christian groups deemed less obedient to the teachings of enslavement and more concerned with spiritual ascension, such as the Cathars. Later, the Muslims tried to do the same to every other group, including Christians and Jews. Every single religion that comes from the same lineage ends up becoming the exact opposite of what it claims to be - not a religion of love and wisdom, but of genocide and intolerance.

The improvement proposed by Islam is blind obedience compared to Christianity, which is another more oppressive form of obedience compared to Judaism. Judaism, in turn, departs from the more scientific, spiritual and ethical approach to spirituality found in the mystic schools of Egypt. Each new religion promoted by these ETs seeks to be more oppressive, intolerant, ignorant, and repressive than the previous one. And blind obedience to these gods then justifies the slaughter of innocents. That is why when Israel bombs Palestine and murders thousands of children, as we see now and in the past years, the rest of the world, especially those of Christian or Jewish descent, remain silent and protest only when a country dominated by their religious ideology is attacked. This hypocrisy and contempt for innocent life, namely children, clearly shows us what these religions truly represent.

Chapter 26: God's Cruelty

Anyone with a discerning mind should recognize the cruelty of the biblical God when they read passages such as Joshua 10:40: "He left none, but utterly destroyed all that breathed, as the LORD God of Israel commanded. According to the Bible, the natives of this region were sentenced to death simply for disobeying God. This justified the more obedient Hebrews in being chosen as Jehovah's favorites. If those who read such things in their holy books see nothing wrong and even think these actions are justified, then the followers of this God are surely in a psychotic state themselves.

If we go along with the thinking of many modern Christians in the United States and Zionists in Israel and assume that Caucasians are more true to their origin as God's people or the ideal slaves, then we must also assume that Caucasians, who are most similar in appearance to this Jehovah group of beings, differ from other humans in that they are the most cruel, obedient, stupid, and easily manipulated. This means that Caucasians have less potential to ascend and leave Earth. However, it also means that they are the apex predators best suited to inherit an Earth run by such aliens.

This places Caucasians at the bottom of the human hierarchy, not the top, no matter how violent they have been to others. The lack of compassion in Caucasians is evidence of their lowest spiritual state.

The true nature and abilities of every spiritual being have been obscured by doctrines that state that only a Supreme Being can enjoy pure spiritual existence and unlimited spiritual potential, and that this Supreme Being has white skin. As a result, we see racism even in cultures where it makes no sense, since evolution has caused the physical characteristics of these people to develop darker skin, thicker hair, and wider noses as a means of protection from sunlight and adaptation to tropical humidity.

This mindset redirects the possibilities and opportunities that people already have within themselves to an external source, limiting them based only on religion and appearance. They then become vulnerable to any spiritual manifestation and scientific trick that can be used against them, either by a foreign entity or by others with such power and technology. This state of mind not only denies people their own spiritual potential for enlightenment, but also keeps them in a perpetual reincarnation loop, especially because they are told that reincarnation is an evil trick and not real, so they will not investigate the subject for fear of repercussions. It is the same attitude that the slaves in Eden had when they were told that wisdom was a bad thing.

How out of touch do you have to be to think that wisdom is evil? Those who still believe this are not far from the primates in the jungle. This kind of illusion puts people at the mercy of their preachers, who, not surprisingly, often abuse such power, either by extorting large sums of money from their followers or by raping the women and children.

The Abrahamic religions have become a sophisticated form of mass manipulation, allowing the use of advanced technology to exploit the gullible fantasies of the masses and their childlike expectations. In doing so, it has prevented people from accessing the true knowledge within themselves and made them completely uninterested in reading anything that is not within the covers of their religious book. Religion has become synonymous with stupidity, ignorance of one's own soul, and blind faith. This is despite the abundance of evidence describing the Abrahamic God as an extraterrestrial being.

For example, the Old Testament says, "There was thunder and lightning and a thick cloud on the mountain, and the sound of the trumpet was very loud; and all the people who were in the camp trembled. Then Moses led the people out of the camp to meet God, and they stood at the foot of the mountain. And Mount Sinai was completely covered with smoke, because the Lord had descended upon it in fire; and the smoke of the fire went up like the smoke of a furnace, and the whole mountain trembled greatly" (Exodus 19:16).

You can believe in flying clouds and fire from which a god descends, if you prefer the fantasy version, or you can grow beyond your childish brain and see it for what it is: UFO technology. This UFO technology produced certain sounds described as "lightning and the sound of a trumpet" (Exodus 19:16). These scriptures also give us a clear description of how God traveled in a cloud when they say: "The Lord went before them [the Hebrew tribes] by day in a pillar of cloud to lead them in the way, and by night in a pillar of fire to give them light; he went day and night; he took not away the pillar of cloud by day, nor the pillar of fire by night, from before the people" (Exodus 13:21-22).

Clearly, the pillar of fire here refers to the lights coming from inside the craft, for the appearance of such fire, as in the lights of the craft, seems to be mentioned in many accounts of God's presence. Thus, the followers of the Abrahamic fantasies have been deceived into praying for their own enslavement, as evidenced by the "sheep mentality" they reinforce in their congregations and when they claim that God is their shepherd. Imagine a religion where people repeat on a weekly basis, "I am an ignorant being without free will, and God guides me because I cannot think for myself; I am just a dumb sheep.

The songs and mantras of the Abrahamic religions may not sound so obvious, but in one way or another they fall into this premise. The cannibalistic ritual of drinking wine as if it were blood and eating bread as if it were the body of Jesus also has little to do with admiration for a man's teachings and much to do with disrespect for his existence. Those who would tell you otherwise are trying to convince you that the best way to remember you after your death is to pretend to eat your body and drink your blood.

What if you were murdered with a stick, and instead of remembering your image, people used the weapon that killed you to celebrate your death? And what if your name was Emmanuel and they decided to call you a pig instead? Because that's what Jesus means in Latin-earth-pig (from the combination of je or ge, which means earth, and sus, which means pig). Then we have the born-again Christians with even more radical absurdities, like the Jehovah's Witnesses, who actually hope for the end of the world to be reborn in paradise. It's like saying, "Please kill us all so we can see how wonderful life after death is. This attitude is not so different from the People's Temple of Jonestown in Guyana, another Abrahamic group of newborn Christians who thought exactly the same thing, isolating themselves from society and trusting no one but their own members before their mass suicide.

Chapter 27: Tactics Exposed

Many consider the Jehovah's Witnesses to be not only another extremist branch of the Abrahamic religions, but also an updated version of a suicide cult. After more than twenty years of interacting with their members and attending their meetings, I have concluded that they employ CIA-level manipulation tactics. They are trained in manipulative mind control methods to recruit new members, and they deliberately lie to attract more people to their group, justifying these lies as acts of faith. They have also become extremely paranoid about anyone from the outside who wants to learn from their group. They conduct intense background checks on everyone's personal life, which goes beyond psychological abuse and easily leads to harassment. They use harassment to control their members. Countless public stories of victims of this group support these observations.

A closer look reveals a very paranoid and apathetic ideology. This is exactly what the followers of this ideology want. They never wage war, but instead welcome wars as a sign that paradise is coming. This sadistic pleasure in war is disturbing from a psychological point of view, but it is not as alarming as the broader panorama of the newborn Christians, which goes beyond the limits of absurdity. The new forms of Christianity are nothing more than updates of mass brainwashing, taking people back to outdated and absurd views of Christianity and making them behave like apathetic sheep worshipping a sacrificial figure while celebrating with the weapon that killed him and pretending to eat his body. If I were a psychopath and wanted to create a religion, this one would seem just fine. It includes cannibalism, blood-drinking rituals, mocking a prophet by celebrating his death, and a bunch of people repeating self-degrading mantras and songs.

The Roman Empire could not defeat the Christians of antiquity by slaughtering them, so it had to defeat them from within by corrupting the religion. Today's Christianity, with all its branches of mass illusionism, has little to do with the original Christian teachings. However, as I have seen, the vast majority of people are not interested in the truth. This truth shows us that all their gods are man-made references to extraterrestrials, although there is a God as a living consciousness in the universe, a Creator who unites the many interplanetary families. This idea is rejected in favor of a certain group of beings who feed on the sick delusions of humans. They are so far removed from reality that they even believe that the five-pointed star, a symbol seen everywhere in nature and especially in flowers, is a symbol of devil worship.

Many interpretations of God still hide extraterrestrial interference because people are too immature and underdeveloped to deal with reality. They even laugh at the possibility of ET interference, as if it makes more sense for them to believe in flying clouds with shining lights. Many of the allegories and assumptions in religious books are fantasies that better represent the human imaginary world and are therefore at their low cognitive level. In religion, as in many other subjects, because the masses are ignorant, they tend to oversimplify what they can't understand or accept. It is like having hundreds of colors and calling them all black or white. But the scriptures are very clear. For example, the book of Genesis says, "Those who came down from heaven and created man," not "God who came down from heaven. It also says, "Let us make them in our image" (Genesis 1:26), in the plural, not the singular. These sentences should be enough to assume that there is a plurality of gods and a Supreme Being whom we also call God, the Creator of the universe and the planets.

In their obsession with oversimplification, humans have lumped everything into the same category, to the point of describing Satan and God in the same book, with interchangeable roles. Humanity did the same thing when it created many names for this god, confusing him with Enki and then inventing a figure named Jesus to symbolize the reincarnation of this sun god. The level of cognitive impairment is so incredible that people are unable to see their own limitations and instead insult and label as arrogant and a blasphemer anyone who shows the obvious: that most adults are too stupid to understand the things they say or their own books, which they often misinterpret and study incorrectly, just like a child with learning disabilities. The difference is that the child has adults to correct him, while adults do not accept to be corrected by anyone.

God, as the creator of the Hindu scriptures, created the earth and the many planets of the universe, and then humans were created by extraterrestrials, as science and archaeology have already proven, to be their slaves. Before this ET interference, there were already humans on Earth, probably much more advanced in consciousness, but not so determined to be enslaved and work for their survival while paying taxes without questioning the purpose of it, as so many do today and always have in the past. Many people will even tell you that a life without sacrifice is not a life dedicated to God, or that not working is not a spiritual thing, because they are so conditioned by their genetic implants that they can't see anything beyond a state of servitude to nonsense.

Chapter 28: Ascension and Slavery

If humans were enlightened, they would instead build a society of robots and other machines to work for them, and devote their time to intellectual and spiritual pursuits through art, music, and study, as advanced civilizations are supposed to do. Instead, science often parallels human ignorance in denying external interference and the need to question our past in order to move in a new direction, rather than being passive observers of a world designed for us and maintained with blind faith. Humanity has a long way to go, but it remains closer to its own enslavement than to evolution, especially because many are trying to use science to keep humanity enslaved.

Salvation today is only at the individual level and comes through discernment and the sacrifice of emotional ideals, namely the need for companionship and a sense of belonging to a group. This humility is the only path to ascension and liberation from the imprisonment that planet Earth represents. It begins with the acceptance that we are immortal beings, and that Earth isn't the only inhabited planet, but one of many billions of planets on which we can be reborn. As an awakened spirit, we should first work towards our liberation on this planet through the acquisition of true knowledge, and then ascend to other realms where we are free from the suffering and ignorance that makes life on earth what it is. The opposite path is always a step away from totalitarian regimes, as we have seen many times in human history.

We have seen what happened with the coronavirus. It was a bioweapon created by powerful and greedy individuals and unleashed on others to destroy economies and change the political theater of the world while targeting undesirable groups of society. And because people are immersed in fear and religious dogma, they cooperated, often with the support of their own preachers who led them to take a mind-altering and DNA-altering vaccine - the mark of the Beast God, the mark of sin or enslavement.

People are so immersed and dependent on the system they know as normal that they can't live without it. They are afraid of dying, of losing their jobs, of not having friends and family to support them emotionally, of being labeled crazy and ostracized by society, and the very fear of disagreeing with this madness makes them as vulnerable as cattle. People have become afraid of not being integrated into a lie, into a herd mentality, because they know no other alternative. That is why no conspiracy will ever be accepted if it is presented against the fear of discrimination.

Those in power have found fear to be the best tool to manipulate the masses, and that's why religion still uses fear to gather a large following. But fear is the path to darkness because fear limits our cognitive abilities and therefore our ability to question and understand ourselves. This condition keeps us trapped on this planet, unable to ascend to higher realms. It also keeps such individuals from ever being of help to those who work for the liberation of other souls, especially because of the discrimination they impose on non-believers, as if a brown cow is different from a white cow, or a black cow, or the cows can be differentiated based on who is the farmer, and not all cows are subject to the same fate.

True freedom begins when we free ourselves from the shackles of fear and ignorance, but it takes courage to question established structures and seek truth beyond appearances. Humanity has the potential to achieve great things, but it is trapped in a vicious cycle of repeating the same mistakes and not learning the same lessons. Accepting our immortality and understanding that Earth is just one stop on our cosmic journey are essential steps toward spiritual ascension.

The ideal society would be one where each individual is free to explore his or her full potential, where cooperation and love prevail over competition and fear. A world where technology is used to elevate human consciousness, not enslave it. But to achieve this society, each individual must take responsibility for his or her own evolution and seek the truth with courage and determination. The reward is true freedom and ascension to higher spheres. The choice is ours: to remain passive observers or to take control of our destiny.

Glossary of Terms

Abrahamic faiths: The three major monotheistic religions-Judaism, Christianity, and Islam-that trace their origins to the patriarch Abraham. These faiths share common beliefs, such as the worship of a single God and the recognition of Abraham as a key figure.

Arianism: A Christian theological doctrine named after Arius, a fourth-century presbyter who claimed that Jesus Christ was not divine but a created being. Arianism was declared heretical by the Council of Nicaea in 325 AD.

Ascension: The spiritual process of rising to a higher level of consciousness or existence. In the context of this book, it refers to the liberation from the constraints of religious dogma and the attainment of enlightenment.

Biblical God: The deity described in the Bible, often referred to as Jehovah or Yahweh. The book explores the idea that the biblical God may be a representation of extraterrestrial beings rather than a single divine entity.

Christ cult: A term used in the book to describe the religious and cultural phenomenon surrounding the figure of Jesus Christ, emphasizing the manipulative and controlling aspects of organized Christianity.

Consciousness: The state of being aware of one's surroundings and one's existence. The book discusses the concept of awakening consciousness as a means of overcoming religious indoctrination and achieving spiritual liberation.

Council of Nicaea: A council of Christian bishops convened at Nicaea in 325 A.D. to address theological disputes, particularly the nature of Jesus Christ. The council resulted in the Nicene Creed, which affirmed the doctrine of the Trinity.

Deception: The act of misleading or deceiving someone, often for personal gain or manipulation. The book examines various forms of deception within religious institutions and their effects on society.

Enlightenment: A state of spiritual awareness and understanding that transcends ordinary consciousness. The book discusses enlightenment as a goal for those who seek to free themselves from religious dogma.

Extraterrestrial interference: The idea that extraterrestrial beings have influenced human history and religious beliefs. The book suggests that many religious figures and events can be attributed to extraterrestrial intervention.

Belief: To believe in something without proof or evidence. The book examines the role of belief in religious indoctrination and its effect on individual consciousness.

Gnostic teachings: Ancient religious and philosophical movements that emphasized the acquisition of knowledge (gnosis) as a means of spiritual liberation. Gnostic teachings often diverged from mainstream Christian doctrines and were suppressed by the early church.

Ignorance: Lack of knowledge or awareness, often resulting from a deliberate effort to conceal information. This book discusses the role of ignorance in maintaining religious control and preventing spiritual growth.

Jehovah's Witnesses: A Christian denomination known for its door-to-door preaching, distribution of religious literature, and refusal of blood transfusions. This book examines the manipulative tactics used by Jehovah's Witnesses to recruit and control members.

Luciferianism: A religious or philosophical belief system that worships Lucifer, often associated with enlightenment and rebellion against oppressive religious structures. This book discusses historical and contemporary interpretations of Luciferianism.

Microchipping: The practice of implanting microchips in individuals for various purposes, such as identification or tracking. The book explores the ethical and social implications of microchipping and its potential for control and manipulation.

Monotheism: The belief in a single, all-powerful deity. The book discusses the origins and implications of monotheistic religions, particularly in the context of the Abrahamic faiths.

Ninth Circle: An alleged international child-sacrifice cult mentioned in the book, allegedly involving high-ranking officials and religious figures. The Ninth Circle is said to be involved in the ritual abuse and murder of children.

Reincarnation: The belief that the soul or spirit can be reborn in a new physical body after death. The book discusses the concept of reincarnation in various religious and philosophical traditions.

Revelation: The act of uncovering or revealing something previously hidden or unknown. The book explores the concept of revelation in the context of religious texts and the unveiling of hidden truths.

Satanism: A religious or philosophical belief system that worships Satan, often associated with rebellion against traditional religious structures. This book discusses historical and contemporary interpretations of Satanism.

Symbols: Objects or images that represent abstract ideas or concepts. This book explores the significance of religious symbols and their hidden meanings.

Trinity: The Christian doctrine that God is one being in three persons: the Father, the Son (Jesus Christ), and the Holy Spirit. The book explores the historical development and theological debates surrounding the concept of the Trinity.

Vatican: The central governing body of the Roman Catholic Church, located in Vatican City. The book discusses the Vatican's role in religious control and manipulation, as well as its alleged involvement in various conspiracies.

Veil of ignorance: A metaphorical term used to describe the state of being unaware of or uninformed about certain truths, often due to deliberate concealment or manipulation. The book discusses the role of the veil of ignorance in maintaining religious control and preventing spiritual growth.

Book Review Request

D ear reader,

Thank you for purchasing this book! I would love to know your opinion. Writing a book review helps in understanding the readers and also impacts other readers' purchasing decisions. Your opinion matters. Please write a book review!

Your kindness is greatly appreciated!

About the Author

Dan Desmarques is a renowned author with a remarkable track record in the literary world. With an impressive portfolio of 28 Amazon bestsellers, including eight #1 bestsellers, Dan is a respected figure in the industry. Drawing on his background as a college professor of academic and creative writing, as well as his experience as a seasoned business consultant, Dan brings a unique blend of expertise to his work. His profound insights and transformational content appeal to a wide audience, covering topics as diverse as personal growth, success, spirituality, and the deeper meaning of life. Through his writing, Dan empowers readers to break free from limitations, unlock their inner potential, and embark on a journey of self-discovery and transformation. In a competitive self-help market, Dan's exceptional talent and inspiring stories make him a standout author, motivating readers to engage with his books and embark on a path of personal growth and enlightenment.

Also Written by the Author

1. 66 Days to Change Your Life: 12 Steps to Effortlessly Remove Mental Blocks, Reprogram Your Brain and Become a Money Magnet

2. A New Way of Being: How to Rewire Your Brain and Take Control of Your Life

3. Abnormal: How to Train Yourself to Think Differently and Permanently Overcome Evil Thoughts

4. Alignment: The Process of Transmutation Within the Mechanics of Life

5. Audacity: How to Make Fast and Efficient Decisions in Any Situation

6. Beyond Belief: Discovering Sacred Moments in Everyday Life

7. Beyond Illusions: Discovering Your True Nature

About the Publisher

This book was published by 22 Lions Publishing.

www.22Lions.com